SPSF

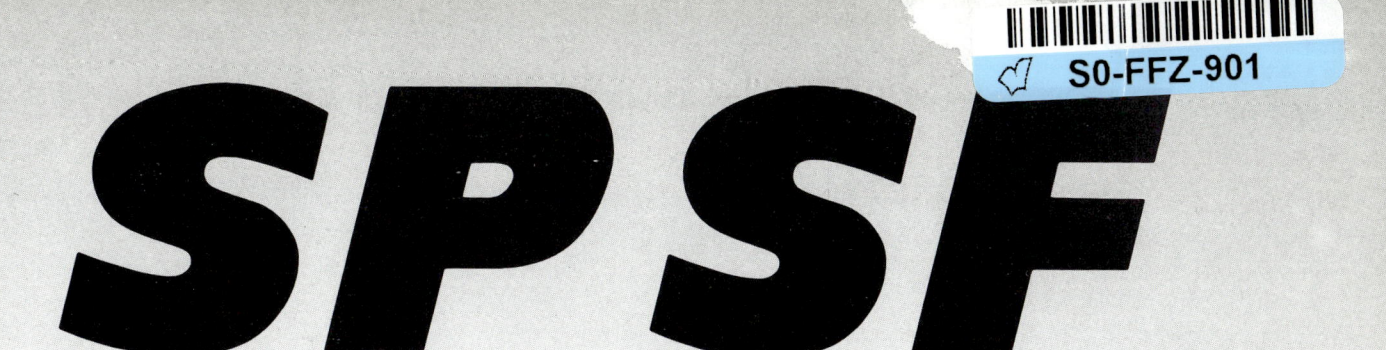

MOTIVE POWER — 1986

By Joseph W. Shine

ACKNOWLEDGEMENTS

The cover of this first edition of SPSF Motive Power is from a transparency taken by my son, John, of Santa Fe's "Museum Train" headed by newly rebuilt SD45-2's, 7207-7206-7205 at Homer in the California desert, west of Needles, on April 1, 1986. The Santa Fe had donated thirteen pieces of historic motive power to the California State Railroad Museum, and the train was enroute from Albuquerque, N.M. to Sacramento.

BACK COVER

On the rear cover are presented two pieces of motive power pertaining to modern railroad history. The top photo, taken on Sullivan's Curve in Cajon Pass, by Mike Start on August 7, 1985, finds the first unit painted in the red and yellow merger scheme, Santa Fe SD45 #5394, on its inaugural run with the 881 train. Below, is a photograph taken by John L. Shine, of Southern Pacific's first merger painted unit, SD45 #7551, on its initial run east of Colton on the morning of August 24, 1985, leading the LAMFF. Both had white initials, which were subsequently changed to yellow, spaced to accept the second pair when and if the merger transpires.

COLOR PHOTOS

There are thirteen color photos in this edition, lazer enhanced to bring you the sharpest and most true-to-life rendition possible. I am indebted to Mark Denis, Mary Pat Dill, Steve Dunham, David Giglio, Bob Hanggie, Jim Heard, Frank Keller, Mike Lepker, Mike Martin, Mike O'Conner, John Shine, Charlie Slater and Mike Start, for lending their color transparencies for consideration. I only wish I could have used more.

I would like to thank the many people who extended a helping hand to a project which, at first, seemed insurmountable. Some, such as Mark Denis, James "Rick" Doughty, Mike Martin and Don Steen, made their entire photo or negative collection available. I am indebted to Thomas Chenoweth, Bob Gallegos, Paul Lukens, Jerry Shine and Shirley Burman Steinheimer who went out of their way to get "that certain" train or locomotive photograph which was needed to fill a gap. My gratitude is extended to everyone with a photo credit line which identifies the particular photographic talent of each one. Without these people such a project could not have even been envisioned.

Other than the photographers, many people helped with data, and records which proved to be invaluable. Dave Dallner, Richard Fischer and Rod Higbie are among these people, as well as many railroad employees such as Carl Ball, Ed Chapman, Ron Dlouhy, Homer Henry, Robert Heuerman, Monte Johnson, Mike Lepker and Charlie Slater, all of whom helped with much needed data and information.

TITLE PAGE

A special thank you goes to Mike Martin with the Public Relations Department of the Santa Fe Southern Pacific Corporation for valuable information and photographs from company files, as well as many photographs from his own collection. The title page photo was submitted by Mike from company files, which depicts motive power of both roads on the famous Tehachapi Loop at Walong.

A very special thanks to my wife, Gail, who devoted many hours into laying out the pages and paste up of all the layout work.

Covering a large railroad the size of the combined Southern Pacific and Santa Fe is going to require the talents of many people. Assuming the merger will be approved by the Interstate Commerce Commission, we are anticipating a yearly publication covering the motive power of the newly formed railroad. Considering the coverage which will be required, we are soliciting your photographic contributions. Crisp, well-focused and well lit black and white photos are requested for consideration.

Remember, railroad property is private property and entering yards and busy terminals is very dangerous, and strongly discouraged by the railroads without proper permission. Action photography out on the road from different locations is preferred, and photos of Southern Pacific or Santa Fe locomotives on foreign roads, and vice versa, will be of great value.

The author may be contacted by addressing a letter to:

- - - -

Four-Ways West Publications
P.O. Box 1734
La Mirada, California
90637-1734

- - - -

This book is copyrighted 1986 by Four-Ways-West Publications. All rights reserved. This book may not be reproduced in part or in whole without the written permission from the publisher, except in the case of brief quotations embodied in critical reviews. Library of Congress Catalog Card #86-082647; International Standard Book No. 0-9616874-0-1.

CONTENTS

ACKNOWLEDGEMENTS
Page 2

THE SANTA FE LOCOMOTIVE ROSTER
Page 4

THE SOUTHERN PACIFIC/COTTON BELT LOCOMOTIVE ROSTER
Pages 5 & 6

PROPOSED SPSF ROSTER (7/24/86)
Pages 6 & 7

MERGER 1980 & 1983
Pages 9-13

PAINTING & NUMBERING
Pages 14-23

CHANGES AFTER 7/24/86
Pages 24 & 25

MERGER PAINTED LOCOMOTIVE LIST
Page 26

ATSF POOL POWER/RUN THROUGHS
Pages 27-30

SP POOL POWER/RUN THROUGHS
Pages 31-36

LOCOMOTIVE TESTING & MOTIVE POWER REQUIREMENTS
Pages 37-40

ICC DECISION 7/24/86
Page 41

1986 - ROSTER IN PHOTOS
Pages 42-128

THE SLUGS
Pages 42-46

THE SWITCHERS
Pages 47-53

EMD 4-AXLE POWER
Pages 54-79

EMD 6-AXLE POWER
Pages 80-113

GE 4-AXLE POWER
Pages 114-121

GE 6-AXLE POWER
Pages 122-128

The Santa Fe roster on this page and Southern Pacific/Cotton Belt roster beginning on page 5, represent the locomotive numbers on each road as of July 24, 1986, the date the Interstate Commerce Commission disapproved the merger of the two carriers. As you will notice, some renumbering of locomotives had already begun. This renumbering is explained on pages 15 and 16.

Throughout the book an asterisk (*) has been used to indicate that the numbers in a series or class are not consecutive.

The page number for each type of locomotive is listed in the right column for easy reference.

THE SANTA FE LOCOMOTIVE ROSTER

AT&SF LOCOMOTIVE NO'S	QUAN.	WHEEL	TYPE	PAGE
101-109,115-119	14	B-B	Slug (Yard)	43
120-121	2	B-B	Slug (Yard)	43
123-125	3	B-B	Slug (Yard)	43
126-129	4	C-C	Slug (Hump)	44
140,145,146	3	C-C	Slug (Hump)	43
141-144	4	C-C	Slug (Hump)	43
1310-1329	20	B-B	GP7 (Reblt)	55
1453	1	B-B	SW900	47
1460	1	B-B	Baldwin/GP7	50
1556-1575	20	C-C	SD39 (Reblt)	87
2000-2027,2050-2062, 2064-2067,2069-2072, 2074-2089,2091-2098, 2100-2109,2111-2115, 2117-2132,2134-2243	214	B-B	GP7 (Reblt)	55
2244-2247,2250-2289, 2291-2299	53	B-B	GP9 (Reblt)	60
2300-2322,2324-2351, 2353-2360	59	B-B	GP38 (Reblt)	70
2370-2380	11	B-B	GP38-2	70
2474,2476,2478-2479, 2482-2484,2488,2493, 2496,2501,2503-2505, 2507,2520,2530,2535, 2537,2541-2542,2544-2545,2548-2550,2561, 2564,2566,2570,2573, 2577-2578,2585-2586, 2589,2591,2596,2598, 2600,2606-2607,2609, 2614,2616,2618-2619, 2621-2624,2629,2633, 2636-2637,2640-2641, 2643-2644,2646,2648	61	B-B	CF7	54
2700-2705,2707-2729, 2731-2748,2750-2757, 2759-2760,2762-2765, 2767-2785	80	B-B	GP30 (Reblt)	65
2814,2818,2823,2830-2832,2840-2894, 2896-2925,2927-2949, 2951-2964	128	B-B	GP35 (Reblt)	68
3000-3010,3012-3026, 3028-3036,3038-3041, 3043-3074	71	B-B	GP20 (Reblt)	63
3100-3121,3123-3124 3126-3130,3132-3151, 3154-3157,3159, 3162-3164,3166-3167, 3170-3172,3175, 3177-3181,3183-3185,				
3189,3194-3197 3199-3201	80	B-B	GP39-2	72
3561-3572,3574-3575, 3577-3579,3581-3586, 3590-3596	30	B-B	GP35 (Reblt)	68
3654,3659,3661-3662, 3669-3670,3673,3676, 3678,3684,3688, 3690-3691,3693-3696, 3701,3705	18	B-B	GP39-2	72
3800-3809	10	B-B	GP40X	77
3810-3854	45	B-B	GP50	78
4600-4601,4603-4607, 4612-4613,4617-4618, 4627,4640-4641,4644-4646,4648,4650,4652, 4655,4657,4661,4665, 4667-4670,4673-4679	35	C-C	SD26 (Reblt)	83
5000-5010,5012-5014, 5016-5019	18	C-C	SD40 (Reblt)	89
5020-5036,5038-5192, 5200-5213	186	C-C	SD40-2	90
5250-5267	18	C-C	SDF40-2	97
5300-5408,5426-5437	121	C-C	SD45 (Reblt)	103
5501-5502	2	C-C	SD45B (Reblt)	104
5626-5627,5633,5636-5639,5645,5651,5656, 5664,5667-5668,5670, 5673-5674,5676,5679, 5683-5684,5689,5693-5694,5698,5700-5701, 5703,5705,5707-5714	36	C-C	SD45-2	108
5950-5989	40	C-C	SDF45 (Reblt)	106
5990-5993,5995-5998	8	C-C	SDFP45 (Reblt)	107
6300,6304-6305,6309, 6311,6313-6319, 6322-6323,6325-6330, 6332-6338,6340, 6342-6345,6347-6348	34	B-B	U23B	114
6350-6418	69	B-B	B23-7	115
7200-7229	30	C-C	SD45-2 (Reblt)	108
7400-7402	3	B-B	B39-8	121
7484-7499	16	B-B	B36-7	120
8010-8166	157	C-C	C30-7	123
8736-8762	27	C-C	U36C	126
9500-9553	54	C-C	SF30C (Reblt)	128

THE SOUTHERN PACIFIC/COTTON BELT LOCOMOTIVE ROSTER

SP/SSW LOCOMOTIVE NO'S	QUAN.	WHEEL	TYPE	PAGE
1010-1013	4	B-B	Slug (Yard)	43
1191-1199	9	B-B	SW900 (Reblt)	47
1307,1311,1321,1324, 1326,1331,1336-1337	8	B-B	NW2 (Reblt)	48
1500-1542	43	C-C	SD7 (Reblt)	80
1600-1613	14	B-B	Slug (Road)	46
2250-2261 (SSW) 2262-2264,2266-2272, 2274-2278,2280-2288 2289-2290 (SSW)	38	B-B	SW1200	48
2294-2296	3	B-B	SW7 (Reblt)	48
2298-2300,2302	4	B-B	SW9 (Reblt)	48
2303	1	B-B	SW1200 (Reblt)	50
2305-2306	2	B-B	SW9 (Reblt)	48
2307	1	B-B	SW1200 (Reblt)	50
2308	1	B-B	SW9 (Reblt)	48
2309-2316	8	B-B	SW1200 (Reblt)	50
2450-2454,2456-2462, 2464-2480 2481-2492 (SSW) 2493-2508,2510 2511-2522 (SSW) 2523-2528,2530-2540, 2542-2578 2579-2590 (SSW) 2591-2642,2644-2674, 2676-2689	233	B-B	SW1500	50
2690-2701	12	B-B	MP15	50
2702-2722,2724-2759	57	B-B	MP15AC	53
2868,2870,2872-2875, 2876-2879, (Reblt) 2884,2887, (Reblt) 2888-2889, 2892, (Reblt) 2893-2894 2897-2899	20	B-B	GP9 (Reblt)	57
2961-2970	10	C-C	SD35 (Reblt)	84
2971-2976	6	C-C	SD38-2	85
3100	1	B-B	U25B (Reblt)	114
3102-3103,3105	3	C-C	SD35 (Reblt)	84
3106-3109	4	C-C	SD35	84
3186-3196	11	B-B	GP9 (Reblt)	57
3197-3199	3	B-B	GP40P-2	74
3200-3209	10	C-C	SDP45	98
3301,3303,3305,3307- 3308,3311-3312,3314, 3316-3317,3319-3320, 3322-3323,3325, 3327-3329,3332-3336, 3338-3345,3347-3350, 3352-3353,3355-3364, 3366-3370,3372-3380, 3382-3385,3387-3388, 3392,3394-3419,3421, 3425-3426,3428-3430, 3432-3436,3438-3441	109	B-B	GP9 (Reblt)	57
3640, 3648 (SSW), 3663,3708-3709,3727	6	B-B	GP9	57
3732-3740,3742-3746, 3748-3751,3753-3757, 3759-3775,3777-3780, 3782-3797,3800-3805, 3808-3813 (SSW), 3816-3817,3819, 3821-3846,3848-3859, 3871,3873 (SSW), 3877-3880,3882-3885	123	B-B	GP9 (Reblt)	57
4060,4063,4079,4085, 4087	5	B-B	GP20	62
4102-4109,4111-4122, 4124-4125, 4134-4135,4137 (SSW), 4139-4144 (SSW), 4146-4153 (SSW)	39	B-B	GP20 (Reblt)	62
4160, 4200-4203 (SSW)	5	B-B	GP35 (Reblt)	66
4301-4307,4310-4320, 4322-4356,4358-4367, 4369-4380,4382-4387, 4389-4413,4415-4441, 4450-4451	135	C-C	SD9 (Reblt)	81
4800-4844	45	B-B	GP38-2	71
5002-5005 (SSW), 5007,5009 (SSW), 5010-5013,5015-5017	13	B-B	GP30	64
5100-5114	15	B-B	B23-7	116
5300,5302,5304,5306, 5308-5310,5314-5318	12	C-C	SD39	86
6300,6302-6361	61	B-B	GP35 (Reblt)	66
6501-6505,6507-6508, 6511,6513-6514, 6516-6517,6519 (SSW) 6521-6523,6526-6527, 6533,6537-6538, 6543-6544,6547, 6551-6552,6554-6556, 6563-6564,6566,6568, 6570,6574,6576-6577, 6579,6582,6584-6585, 6587-6590,6593,6595, 6597,6600,6604-6607, 6609,6611,6614,6615, 6617,6619-6620,6622- 6623,6628,6631,6632, 6639-6640,6643-6646, 6650,6652-6653,6657, 6660-6661,6666,6668- 6671,6674,6676,6679 6680-6681 (SSW)	87	B-B	GP35	66
6767,6769-6771	5	C-C	SD45T-2 (Reblt)	110
7200-7201,7230-7231	4	B-B	GP40X	76
7240-7247	48	B-B	GP40-2	75
7248-7273 (SSW)	25	B-B	GP40-2	75
7300-7346,7348-7385	85	B-B	SD40 (Reblt)	88
7399	1	B-B	SD45 (Reblt)	100
7400-7566	167	B-B	SD45 (Reblt)	100
7608-7611,7613-7619, 7621-7627 7628-7642 (SSW) 7644-7645 (SSW) 7647-7657 (SSW) 7658-7677	66	B-B	GP40-2	75
7754-7769	16	B-B	B36-7	118
7770,7772-7773 (SSW)	3	B-B	B36-7	118
7771 (SSW)	1	B-B	B36-7B	118

7774-7799 (SSW)		26	B-B	B30-7	117
7801-7809,7811-7853, 7855-7883		81	B-B	B30-7	117
7940-7956,7958-7959		19	B-B	GP40-2M	73
7960-7967 (SSW)		8	B-B	GP40M (Reblt)	73
8230-8299		70	C-C	SD40T-2	93
8300-8301,8303-8321		21	C-C	SD40T-2(M)	
8322-8326 (SSW)		5	C-C	SD40T-2(M)	
8327-8341		15	C-C	SD40T-2(M)	
8350-8371		22	C-C	SD40T-2(R)	
8372-8376 (SSW)		5	C-C	SD40T-2(R)	
8377-8391		15	C-C	SD40T-2(R)	93
8489-8573		85	C-C	SD40T-2	93
8585-8586,8588-8599, 8653,8662,8669,8673, 8689,8698,8703-8705, 8712,8717,8720,8725, 8727,8754,8756,8760, 8762,8771-8773, 8776-8777,8780		38	C-C	U33C	122
8818,8822,8859,8872, 8874,8887,8889,8898, 8900,8909-8910,8925, 8927,8933,8935-8937, 8939,8942,8944,8951, 8953,8955-8956,8958-8962, 8965,8968 (SSW) 8978,8981 (SSW), 8988,8990,8992-8993, 8996-8997,9000,9002, 9007,9013,9015,9016-9017,9019,9021,9023-9025,9027,9030-9031, 9034,9036-9037,9040-9042,9047,9049, 9052,9055 (SSW) 9065-9066,9068 (SSW), 9071,9074-9075,9080, 9081-9083,9085-9088, 9092,9095-9100, 9104-9105,9107-9110, 9115-9116,9120-9121, 9123-9125,9127-9130, 9132,9135,9137-9140, 9151, 9155 (SSW)		109	C-C	SD45	100
9157-9159 (SSW), 9161-9162 (SSW), 9164-9165 (SSW), 9166-9167,9170,9172, 9175,9179,9181-9183, 9185,9187-9190, 9192-9195,9197-9198, 9201-9203,9206-9209, 9211-9215,9217-9219, 9221-9224,9226-9247, 9249-9250,9253-9254, 9256-9257,9259-9260, 9261-9279 (SSW), 9282-9289 (SSW), 9291-9301 (SSW), 9302-9353,9355-9370, 9371-9378 (SSW), 9380-9404 (SSW)		215	C-C	SD45T-2	110
9501		1	C-C	SD45T-2 (Reblt)	110

THE SPSF LOCOMOTIVE ROSTER

This SPSF Locomotive Roster is based on the roster as of July 24, 1986, the date the Interstate Commerce Commission denied the merger. Some changes have already taken place, and if the merger is finally approved, more changes will have taken place. As locomotives are retired and/or sold the numbers shift, and as older units are remanufactured, new number series are acquired. This proposed roster is presented as a guide only.

SPSF	PREVIOUS NO'S	TYPE	QUAN.	PAGE
100-103	SP 1010-1013	Slug (Yard)	4	43
104-105	ATSF 120-121	Slug (Yard)	2	43
106-108	ATSF 123-125	Slug (Yard)	4	43
109-112	ATSF 116-119	Slug (Yard)	4	43
113-116	ATSF 101-103,115	Slug (Yard)	4	43
117-122	ATSF 104-109	Slug (Yard)	6	43
150-156	ATSF 140-146	Slug (Hump)	7	43
157-160	ATSF 126-129	Slug (Hump)	4	44
200-213	SP 1600-1613	Slug (TEBU)	14	46
Electro-Motive Division				
300	ATSF 1453	SW900	1	47
301-309	SP 1191-1199	SW900 Reblt	9	47
310-317	SP 1307-1337*	NW2E	8	48
318-329	SSW 2250-2261	SW1200	12	48
330-353	SP 2262-2288*	SW1200	24	48
354-355	SSW 2289-2290	SW1200	2	48
356-358	SP 2294-2296	SW7 Reblt	3	48
359-361	SP 2298-2300	SW9 Reblt	3	48
362-366	SP 2312-2316	SW1200 Reblt	5	50
367-370	SP 2302-2308*	SW9 Reblt	4	48
371-375	SP 2303-2311*	SW1200 Reblt	5	50
600	ATSF 1460	GP/Bald	1	50
601-629	SP 2450-2480*	SW1500	29	50
630-642	SSW 2481-2492	SW1500	12	50
643-659	SP 2493-2510*	SW1500	17	50
660-672	SSW 2511-2522	SW1500	12	50
673-726	SP 2523-2578*	SW1500	54	50
727-738	SSW 2579-2590	SW1500	12	50
739-835	SP 2591-2689*	SW1500	99	50
900-911	SP 2690-2701	MP15	12	50
912-940	SP 2702-2731*	MP15AC	29	53
941-964	SP 2736-2769	MP15AC	24	53
965-968	SP 2732-2735	MP15AC	4	53
1000-1060	ATSF 2474-2648*	CF7	61	54
1100-1119	ATSF 1310-1329	GP7 Reblt	20	55
1200-1227	ATSF 2000-2027	GP7 Reblt	28	55
1228-1413	ATSF 2050-2243	GP7 Reblt	186	55
1500-1542	SP 1500-1542	SD7	43	80
1550-1555	SP 2971-2976	SD38-2	6	85
1556-1575	ATSF 4000-4019	SD39 Reblt	20	87
1576-1579	SP 3106-3109	SD35	4	84
1580-1582	SP 3102,03,05	SD35 Reblt	3	84
1583-1592	SP 2961-2970	SD35 Reblt	10	84
1599	SP 3100	U25B Reblt	1	114

6

1700-1701	SP 2877,3640	GP9	2	57
1702	SSW 3648	GP9	1	57
1703-1704	SP 2889,3663	GP9	2	57
1705-1706	SP 2879,2888	GP9	2	57
1707-1708	SP 2894,2893	GP9	2	57
1709-1710	SP 2876,2878	GP9	2	57
1711-1712	SP 3708-3709	GP9	2	57
1713	SP 3727	GP9	1	57
1717-1936*	SP 2868-2899*	GP9 Reblt	12	57
1714-1829*	SP 3301-3441*	GP9 Reblt	109	57
1830-1898*	SP 3732-3805*	GP9 Reblt	66	57
1899-1904	SSW 3808-3813	GP9 Reblt	6	57
1905-1946*	SP 3816-3859*	GP9 Reblt	41	57
1947-1948	SSW 3871,3873	GP9 Reblt	2	57
1949-1959	SP 3186-3196	GP9 Reblt	11	57
1960-1967	SP 3877-3885*	GP9 Reblt	8	57
1968-2020	ATSF 2244-2299*	GP9 Reblt	53	60
2300-2358	ATSF 2300-2360*	GP38 Reblt	59	70
2400-2410	ATSF 2370-2380	GP38-2	11	70
2411-2455	SP 4800-4844	GP38-2	45	71
2795-2799	SP 4060-4087*	GP20	5	62
2800-2821	SP 4102-4125*	GP20 Reblt	22	62
2822-2837	SSW 4134-4153*	GP20 Reblt	16	62
2838-2908	ATSF 3000-3074*	GP20 Reblt	71	62
2950	SP 4160	GP35 Reblt	1	66
2951-2954	SSW 4200-4203	GP35 Reblt	4	66
3000-3005	SSW 5002-5009*	GP30	6	64
3006-3012	SP 5010-5017*	GP30	7	64
3100-3202	ATSF 3600-3705*	GP39-2	103	72
3300-3379	ATSF 2700-2785*	GP30 Reblt	80	65
3400-3412	SSW 6501-6519*	GP35	13	66
3413-3486	SP 6521-6679*	GP35	74	66
3487-3488	SSW 6680-6681	GP35	2	66
3500-3560	SP 6300-6361*	GP35 Reblt	61	66
3561-3718	ATSF 2801-2964*	GP35 Reblt	158	68
4000-4018	SP 7940-7959*	GP40-2M	19	73
4019-4026	SSW 7960-7967	GP40M Reblt	8	73
4100-4102	SP 3197-3199	GP40P-2	3	74
4103-4121	SP 7608-7627*	GP40-2	19	75
4122-4149	SSW 7628-7657*	GP40-2	28	75
4150-4169	SP 7658-7677	GP40-2	20	75
4170-4177	SP 7240-7247	GP40-2	8	75
4178-4203	SSW 7248-7273	GP40-2	26	75
4400-4403	SP 7200,01,30,31	GP40X	4	76
4404-4413	ATSF 3800-3809	GP40X	10	77
4500-4544	ATSF 3810-3854	GP50	45	78
5000-5134	SP 4301-4451*	SD9 Reblt	136	81
5300-5311	SP 5300-5318*	SD39	12	86
5400-5434	ATSF 4600-4679*	SD26 Reblt	35	83
5500	SP 7399	SD45 Reblt	1	101
5501-5585	SP 7300-7385*	SD40 Reblt	85	88
5586-5603	ATSF 5000-5019*	SD40 Reblt	18	89
5700-5706 Even	ATSF 5020-5026	SD40-2	4	90
5701-5707 Odd	ATSF 5021-5027	SD40-2	4	90
5708-5738 Even	ATSF 5110-5140	SD40-2	16	90
5709-5739 Odd	ATSF 5109-5139	SD40-2	16	90
5740-5780 Even	SP 8300-8321*	SD40T-2	21	93
5741-5783 Odd	SP 8350-8356	SD40T-2	22	93
5782-5790 Even	SSW 8322-8326	SD40T-2	5	93
5785-5793 Odd	SSW 8372-8376	SD40T-2	5	93
5792-5820 Even	SP 8327-8341	SD40T-2	15	93
5795-5823 Odd	SP 8377-8391	SD40T-2	15	93
5825-5909	SP 8489-8573	SD40T-2	85	93
5910-5979	SP 8230-8299	SD40T-2	70	93
6000-6028	ATSF 5028-5057*	SD40-2	29	90
6029-6042	SP 5200-5213	SD40-2	14	90
6043-6093	ATSF 5058-5108	SD40-2	51	90
6094-6145	ATSF 5141-5192	SD40-2	52	90
6300-6325	SP 8818-8962*	SD45	26	100
6326-6329	SSW 8965-8981*	SD45	4	100
6330-6358	SP 8988-9049*	SD45	29	100
6359-6363	SSW 9052-9068*	SD45	5	100
6364-6404	SP 9071-9151*	SD45	41	100
6405	SSW 9155	SD45	1	100
6406-6413	SP 3200-3209*	SDP45 (Frt)	8	98
6500-6517	ATSF 5250-5267	SDF40-2Rblt	18	97
6550-6589	ATSF 5950-5989	SDF45 Reblt	40	106
6600-6766	SP 7400-7566	SD45 Reblt	167	101
6767	SP 9500 (SSW 9163)	SD45T-2 Rblt	1	111
6768	SP 9501 (SP 9171)	SD45T-2 Rblt	1	111
6769-71	SP 9180,9196,9200	SD45T-2 Rblt	3	111
6950-6961	ATSF 5426-5437	SD45 Reblt	12	103
6990-6991	ATSF 5501-5502	SD45B Reblt	2	104
7000-7108	ATSF 5300-5408	SD45 Reblt	109	103
7200-7233	ATSF 5625-5704*	SD45-2 Rblt	34	109
7300-7335	ATSF 5625-5714*	SD45-2	36	108
7600-7606	SSW 9157-9165*	SD45T-2	7	110
7607-7675	SP 9166-9260*	SD45T-2	69	110
7676-7713	SSW 9261-9301*	SD45T-2	38	110
7714-7781	SP 9302-9370*	SD45T-2	68	110
7782-7814	SSW 9371-9404*	SD45T-2	33	110
7900-7901	SP 3201,3207	SDP45 (Pass)	2	99
7990-7997	ATSF 5990-5998*	SDFP45 Reblt	8	107

GENERAL ELECTRIC LOCOMOTIVES

8100-8133	ATSF 6300-6348*	U23B	34	114
8134-8188	ATSF 6350-6404	B23-7	55	115
8189-8203	SP 5100-5114	B23-7	15	116
8204-8217	ATSF 6405-6418	B23-7	14	115
8300-8380	SP 7801-7883*	B30-7	81	117
8381-8482	SSW 7774-7799	B30-7	26	117
8500	SSW 7771	B36-7B	1	118
8501-8503	SSW 7770-7773*	B36-7	3	118
8504-8519	ATSF 7484-7499	B36-7	14	120
8520-8535	SP 7754-7769	B36-7	16	118
	SP 8585-8780*	U33C	36	122
8800-8802	ATSF 7400-7402	B39-8	3	121
9400-9426	ATSF 8736-8762	U36C	27	126
9500-9560	ATSF 8700-8799*	SF30C Reblt	61	128
9700-9854	ATSF 8010-8166	C30-7	157	124

A number of SP SD45T-2's and several Santa Fe SD45-2's, GP39-2's, and U36C's are not listed as they have been retired for remanufacturing programs at the Sacramento Locomotive Works, San Bernardino Shops and Cleburne Shops.

Southern Pacific's GE U33C's were not assigned SPSF numbers.

Series marked with an asterisk (*) are not consecutive.

Shortly after the two corporations began formal talks in 1980, the railroads were asked to set up a photo which would be included in an article in Forbes Magazine pertaining to the anticipated merger. The session was staged at LA's Mission Tower diamonds on Santa Fe's Second District. Southern Pacific regularly operates transfer trains on this trackage between Taylor Yard (SP) and Hobart Yard (AT&SF). The motive power utilized were Southern Pacific GP40X's and Santa Fe CF7's.

Mike Martin/SFSP Corp.

MERGER - 1980

Prior to the spring of 1980, it was unthinkable to envision a Southern Pacific-Santa Fe merger, as the two roads had always competed for routes and traffic from the early days when the pair of giants were building and expanding in the West and Southwest.

Forced to compete in an environment of mega-mergers, beginning in the west with the merger of the lines which formed the Burlington Northern in 1970, and more recently the Union Pacific/Missouri Pacific/Western Pacific (Mop-UP) merger, then pending, as well as the BN-Frisco merger, also pending, it became obvious to management of both roads that a partner must be sought in order to remain competitive. Since deregulation, most railroads have been hurt by over capacity and the loss of revenue from the troubled steel, grain, lumber and automobile sectors, which traditionally account for the bulk of all rail freight.

Thus, the first joint public announcement was issued on May 15, 1980 by Santa Fe's Chairman of the Board and Chief Executive Officer John S. Reed and Southern Pacific's Chairman and CEO Benjamin Biaggini which proclaimed the intention of both corporations.

During June 1980 the first obvious events relating to these talks transpired. First, a power short Santa Fe leased twenty-five 8500 series SD40T-2's from Southern Pacific, in an action unprecedented by the two roads. Prior to this, about the only time motive power from the two roads operated together was in light helper moves in the Tehachapi Mountains to cut down on train movements over the district. As requested by the Southern Pacific these locomotives were operated generally west of Barstow to keep them close to home in case they were required to be returned from this short term lease.

Next, a pair of units, one from the Southern Pacific and one from Santa Fe, were assembled at the laters Hobart Yard (Los Angeles) for photographs for the Public Relations Department files. Also at SP's request, Santa Fe helped set up a publicity photo at Walong (Tehachapi Loop), for their PR Department.

The third event occurred on June 29, 1980 when a pair of spotless SP 8200 series SD40T-2's brought four Southern Pacific business cars including SP 150 "Sunset" into West Colton from the east. After servicing the cars at West Colton, an Espee switcher brought the "Sunset"

During the summer of 1980, while initial merger talks were being held, a power short Santa Fe leased twenty-five SP 8500-series SD40T-2's. Just delivered 8501 and 8508 wait at San Bernardino for a call to duty, while Santa Fe SD26 #4665 waits on an adjacent track.

Mark A. Denis

MERGER - 1983

out to the interchange track at Colton Interlocking where Santa Fe GP35 #3345 brought it to San Bernardino. There, the "Sunset" and Santa Fe's #52 "Atchison" were coupled together for a trip to Chicago behind Amtrak train #4, the Southwest Limited. The 3345 added the pair of business cars to the rear of #4's three SDP40F's and twelve cars headed for the Windy City, where the new corporation's headquarters were to be located. Preliminary talks were held aboard the pair of business cars between officials from both corporations, headed by John Reed and Benjamin Biaggini.

Then, in late August 1980, before a formal proposal was made to the Interstate Commerce Commission, the two roads made a joint announcement indicating that there would be a delay in making a request to the ICC. Talks were broken off and each went their separate way.

Santa Fe also returned SP's twenty-five leased SD40T-2 locomotives at that time.

On November 21, 1980 the Frisco and QA&P were merged into the Burlington Northern. The UP-MP-WP merger was granted on December 22, 1982, and the Santa Fe was entangled in a dispute with the ICC in granting trackage rights to the Denver & Rio Grande Western between Pueblo, Colorado and Kansas City, of which a portion was owned by the Santa Fe. This problem was quickly resolved, the UP/MP/WP became one, and exactly three years after their first courtship ended, Santa Fe Industries and Southern Pacific Transportation announced, once again, their intentions to merge. At that time B. F. Biaggini was still Chairman of the Southern Pacific (he has since retired), and in April John J. Schmidt had taken over control of Santa Fe Industries from John S. Reed, who had retired.

Between the conclusion of talks in 1980 and the new proposals of 1983, all was not quiet on the merger front. The Family Lines and SP had held merger talks, five percent of Santa Fe

On a warm June morning in 1980, Southern Pacific sent SD40T-2 (snoot) #8321 from Taylor Yard (LA) to Santa Fe's Hobart Yard for an official portrait with Santa Fe SD45 #5601.
Mike Martin/SFSP Corp.

If the merger is finally accepted by the ICC, this double track portion of the Santa Fe will carry much of the east/west traffic. Newly installed CTC now makes it possible for bi-directional operation as we see here with an eastbound train (running on the old westbound main) at MP 589, eleven miles west of Needles on February 16, 1985. Many improvements such as this have taken place on both the Southern Pacific and Santa Fe. *Joe Shine*

Industries common stock had been purchased by Norfolk & Western in February 1982 during merger talks (just prior to the N&W-Southern merger), and late in 1982 talks had taken place between the Burlington Northern and Santa Fe. In 1983 Santa Fe was also making moves toward acquiring Conrail, to form the first truly transcontinental railroad. There was even speculation that if the AT&SF/SP merger was swift, a Conrail acquisition proposal might follow shortly.

The parent companies of the two railroads did not need Interstate Commerce Comission approval to merge, so Santa Fe Industries and Southern Pacific Transportation became the Santa Fe Southern Pacific Corportion in December 1983, with the merging of the two railroads in limbo until approval or disapproval came from the ICC.

PREPARING TO MERGE

Plans were quick to be implemented in preparation for the merger, in anticipation of an ICC approval. Many routes which were expected to carry much of the traffic were upgraded and many changes have taken place within the last couple of years. Many were very obvious but some were hardly noticeable.

As an example, much of the traffic from Oregon and northern California bound for the southeast was planned to go through Barstow to Cadiz, California and head down the rehabilitated Parker branch through Phoenix to Tucson and then east. This would have kept many trains out of two helper districts, Cajon and Beaumont, and out of the busy San Bernardino-Colton area.

Many of Santa Fe's older bridges and culverts located east of Barstow were replaced, and some of the double track in the Needles, California area received Centralized Traffic Control (CTC) in order to operate bi-directional on both tracks.

Centralized Traffic Control for the entire San Joaquin Valley for both roads were relocated in the same Fresno, California facility, which considering the ICC disapproval, will make it a very unique situation.

There have been interchange tracks installed between the Southern Pacific and Santa Fe in many locations where just crossings had existed which would have helped facilitate the swift movement of freight. Interchanges like Stockton, Colton and Los Nietos are already in place, and more were planned. There are crossovers at locations near where the tracks of both roads are nearly parallel such as Keenbrook, and there were also crossovers planned for Devore/Dike and Martinez Spur/Hiland, all in Cajon Pass.

Thousands of crossties and hundreds of miles of welded rail had been installed by both roads to improve the physical plant so the "new merged road" would be ready to go after some of the business that had been lost to competition, both rail and truck.

On April 27, 1985, Southern Pacific's Bakersfield-LA "Oil Cans", unit TankTrain, passes over itself on the Tehachapi Loop at Walong, with a combination of Southern Pacific and Santa Fe units. The Santa Fe U36C and SD45 are on lease to the power short Espee. *Joe Shine*

TOGETHER - NOT MERGED

While SP SD40T-2's were on lease to the Santa Fe in the west during the summer of 1980, further east, a Cotton Belt bridge located at Durham, Kansas received heavy fire damage which resulted in detouring many SSW trains over the Santa Fe, between Hutchinson and Kansas City, during their heavy grain rush. To many it appeared as if the two roads were not waiting for ICC's approval to mingle locomotives. This, of course, was not the case.

Shortly after the 1983 announcement, during the first week of October, heavy rains forced the SP to detour many trains between Vaughn, N.M. and Colton or Los Angeles over the Santa Fe to avoid the many washouts throughout Arizona. Many SP units had been caught on the eastern end of the system so the Santa Fe leased eight six-axle units, both EMD and GE, to the SP, four at Bakersfield and four at Colton. The lease was not repaid in dollars but in horsepower hours owed, so after the big blue units were returned, several SP units were handed over to the Santa Fe to operate as repayment.

This detour arrangement and power swap has transpired several times since late 1983, transferring the Southern Pacific onto Santa Fe rails and vice versa, greatly reducing late freight shipments on both roads, thereby enhancing better customer relations. That's what it's all about!

Santa Fe leased several Southern Pacific SD40T-2's during the summer of 1980. AT&SF 3809-SP 8500-8529-8513 (GP40X/3 SD40T-2's) had brought the 308 train (KC-LA) into LA on the 3rd District, LA Division and are returning to Barstow on the 2nd District cab-hop on July 6, 1980. *Mike Martin*

Southern Pacific's MLLAA (Milwaukee Road-LA/Autos) detoured from Vaughn, N.M., via the Santa Fe, due to flood damage on the SP in Arizona during April 1984. The train, led by Santa Fe C30-7 #8161 (with Milw SD40-2 #165 in consist) is leaving the Santa Fe at Broadway (LA) and is heading for SP's Taylor Yard. Motive power problems required Santa Fe CF7 #2485 to shove behind Cotton Belt caboose #72, from Rivera to Taylor Yard.
John L. Shine

Joe Shine

Mid-train helpers on an eastbound Santa Fe train (above), with SP SD40-T-2 #8495 in the consist, work uphill through Bealville in the Tehachapis, while a set of power, (below) consisting of ATSF 5313-SP 8494-8498-ATSF 5689-5980 (SD45/2 SD40T-2's/SD45-2/SDF45) idle in UP's yard in Denver. Southern Pacific's 8489-8498 series SD40T-2's operate on Santa Fe by virtue of a joint coal hauling contract.
John L. Shine

13

PAINTING and NUMBERING

A NEW IMAGE

After preliminary talks were held in 1983, and an official intent to merge was filed with the ICC, the Santa Fe Southern Pacific Corporation began considering the possibility of a new paint scheme for their more than 4000 diesel locomotives. Both Southern Pacific and Santa Fe were asked to submit their ideas for a new scheme. SP's gray and the AT&SF blue were to be discarded and emphasis were to be placed on a more vibrant scheme using SP's red and Santa Fe's yellow as the predominant colors.

Southern Pacific presented their version in writing which consisted of a yellow carbody, black roof extending back from the rear of the yellow cab, SP's standard red wing on the nose and red rear, with a red stripe running along the top of the black frame. It had white handrails, with the SP&SF lettering and cab numbers in black.

Santa Fe acquired the services of Ron Dlouhy, one of their San Bernardino machinists, who is also a very talented model railroader to paint up SP's version plus three Santa Fe versions, including one which was almost identical to the scheme finally adopted. The HO gauge models were sent to Chicago for inspection and a possible decision. The model that was chosen contained red sides and roof with the yellow warbonnet. The model was returned to San Bernardino with the request to paint the roof behind the cab in black. After Chicago made several modifications, Santa Fe's San Bernardino Shops and Southern Pacific's Sacramento Locomotive Works were commissioned to each paint one prototype unit in the newly chosen scheme. The units each road chose to paint was the next in line to be repainted in the their respective rebuilding program. That meant that Santa Fe's unit would be SD45 #5394, and Southern Pacific's would be SD45 #7551.

SANTA FE 5394

The first unit to be painted was Santa Fe's 5394 at San Bernardino on Wednesday July 31, 1985. The unit was first outshopped with a solid yellow nose and black SPSF nose letters, along with large white SPSF side letters. The nose was deemed too drab so by that afternoon the unit again emerged from the paint booth, this time sporting a black nose band with white SPSF letters. A third nose band was tried sporting a red band with four smaller red bands trailing back along the side of the nose with a white SF. Due to problems developing from so much repainting of the nose, the unit was not actually released until August 7th. A color photo of the 5394 is on the back cover.

SP 7551

Southern Pacific's SD45 #7551 was out in the sunlight at the Sacramento Locomotive Works for the company photographer on August 8, 1985. In a move intended to keep rail photographers out of the shop area, SP parked their bright newly painted unit across from the California State Railroad Museum in Old Sacramento from Friday August 9th through Sunday August 11th. The unit was subsequently moved to Eugene, Oregon to be set up for release into general service. A color photo of the 7551 on its first trip east of Colton graces our rear cover.

SANTA FE 5401 & 5402

Subsequent units were released in blue until Santa Fe's 5401 emerged from San Bernardino's booth, during the first week of September, sporting modified nose and side letters in yellow instead of white as on the 5394 and 7551. Further alterations were applied to Santa Fe's 5402, outshopped in mid-September, which was described as the "official" scheme. The 5402 featured a three striped nose band located in a slightly lower position to

After several test schemes with the nose band and four initials on both the sides and nose, the first red and yellow unit, Santa Fe 5394, emerged from San Bernardino's paint booth with the scheme it was finally released in. The "SF" on the sides and nose are in white.
Mike Martin/SFSP Corp.

14

accommodate SP's nose lights, and a raised black roof level to just below the dynamic brake housing, rendering a larger red area on the sides.

Santa Fe's Cleburne, Texas shops and Argentine, Kansas shops continued painting units in the blue/bonnet scheme until November. Early December saw San Bernardino change to the red bonnet scheme. Sacramento painted a few units in the new scheme between November 1985 and January 1986, but everything repainted after mid-January was in the new colors.

RED IN QUANITY

During December Santa Fe's San Bernardino Shops were in the process of rebuilding their rather small fleet of SD39's into slug mothers, and while several had already been released in blue and yellow, all units released after December 2nd were in the new red and yellow scheme. As a matter of fact, the first SD39 painted red, #1569, was actually painted in the blue scheme prior to being released from the shops. It was taken back into the paint booth at San Bernardino, repainted in the red scheme and then released.

The new paint scheme was obviously adopted by Santa Fe, and when applied to SP units a problem developed. The nose band was too high and when (and if) the four initials were adopted the nose lights would have been in the way. On subsequent units this nose stripe was lower.   *Mary Pat Dill*

Santa Fe's Cleburne Shops were remanufacturing their U36C's into SF30C's when their paint shops began repainting everything in the new red scheme. The first SF30C to be outshopped in red was 9510.

Sacramento Locomotive Works was in the midst of rebuilding their large fleet of SD45's when they began repainting every locomotive in the new scheme. SD45's #7400-7550 and 7552-7555 had already been rebuilt and were in the familiar gray and red scheme, but #7556 through 7566 were all in the new red with yellow bonnet scheme.

STANDARDIZATION

Following Santa Fe's practice of removing oscillating headlights, as on their own SDFP45's and SDF40-2's, and installing rotating beacons on all units, SP's rebuilt SD45's above #7562 were outshopped minus "Mars lights", but with amber beacons mounted on the cab roof. The first rebuilt SD45T-2's were also outshopped without gyralights.

Southern Pacific's oscillating headlights had dated back to the steam era when their Daylight GS-4's of 1941 were delivered. All passenger and freight diesels, as well as most switchers and road switchers of the Pacific Lines (West of El Paso), came equipped with these oscillating lights.

Santa Fe style cab numbers, which are similar to SP's (but smaller) were also adopted. Some of the 7561-7566 series, along with other types of units just repainted carry these Santa Fe type numbers.

NEW NUMBERS & PAINT - AT&SF

In May 1985 the first unit to be released with numbers geared to fit into the SPSF system was outshopped from Cleburne. Rebuilt U36C, now designated as a SF30C, carried 9500 in its number boards and on its cab side. The new paint scheme had not yet been chosen, so 9500 through 9509 were outshopped in blue. The same occurred at San Bernardino with the first nine SD39 rebuilds being released in blue, but with numbers in the SPSF 1556 series.

It was believed that the first complete class to be outshopped in the new red and yellow scheme would be Santa Fe's rebuilt SD45-2's in the SPSF 7200 class. There were also a few oddities within the 7200 series. In early June 1986, the 7219 and 7221 were stenciled with the complete "SPSF" nose and hood lettering for official photos. The 7219 was towed onto the mainline to be turned, however, it nor the 7221, was released from San Bernardino with the complete lettering. The 7220 was released from the shops with black instead of silver trucks. Officials were not impressed with this new variation and after only one week on the road the trucks were repainted in the standard silver.

While Santa Fe's rebuilt 1556 class SD39's, 7200 class SD45-2's and 9500 class SF30C's carried post-merger SPSF numbers, the month of June saw the first non-rebuilt units renumbered with their respective SPSF numbers. Most Santa Fe GP39-2's (ATSF 3600-3705*) were renumbered 3100-3202 (SPSF numbers) prior to the ICC decision in July. The second group to be renumbered was the lower numbered 2800 series GP35's (2801-2842*), which became the SPSF 3561-3599 series. Santa Fe's 3000 series GP20's were scheduled to be renumbered in the SPSF 2800 series when ICC's negative decision was announced and consequently none were renumbered. The GP39-2's, GP35's and GP20's were all to be renumbered so the newly rebuilt GP39-2's could fit into the SPSF 3000 series.

NEW NUMBERS & PAINT - SP

As fast as Santa Fe was progressing with their renumbering and repainting, it seemed as if Southern Pacific was moving at a snails pace. Their last eleven rebuilt SD45's (7556-7566) were painted in the red/yellow scheme, plus about eighty more units which were in for general repairs.

SP began remanufacturing their SD45T-2 fleet at the Sacramento Locomotive Works during the second quarter of 1986. The first two, SP 9500 and 9501, were outshopped in April and May in the new scheme, but with strictly Espee numbers. With prompting from Chicago the next rebuilt SD45T-2's were numbered above 6769, while SP 9500 was renumbered 6767. The 9501 was to be renumbered 6768, but it was not done as of late July. In case you are wondering why the rebuilt SD45T-2 numbers began at 6767, it is because their rebuilt SD45's (7400-7566) were to become SPSF 6600-6766.

Enroute to Chicago on its first eastbound trip, the 5394 developed problems in the desert between California and Arizona on August 10, 1985. At Yucca, Arizona the brightly painted unit is being removed from the point. *Don Steen*

While Santa Fe changed their first two red units to conform with the standard, SP merely changed the side and nose initials to yellow from white. At Loma Linda in March of 1986 the 7551 appears much the same as it did when originally painted except for the yellow initials. *John L. Shine*

Santa Fe's second unit outshopped in the new scheme was much the same as the first, except that the 5401 utilized one less color, white. Unlike the 5394, #5401 was kept close to home during its first few trips. The 5401 had worked from San Bernardino to LA, and is now enroute from LA to Barstow. *Mike Martin/SFSP Corp.*

In early July 1986, a pair of SD45-2's, 7219 and 7221, being rebuilt at San Bernardino received the full "SPSF" lettering scheme in preparation for a favorable decision to be rendered by the ICC later in the month. Official photos were to be taken for press packets which were to be distributed to the media during the press release. (Above) The need for one of the units to be turned brought the 7219 (not running) out of the shop area on July 14, 1986.
James Heard

Santa Fe 5402, (right) outshopped in mid-September 1985, contained some modifications to the original merger scheme. The 5402 was photographed at Sullivan's Curve in Cajon Pass on September 20th, displaying these modifications. The nose band and cab numbers have been slightly lowered to accomodate units containing nose lights. The black roof extending down the sides is much higher rendering a larger red area and the nose band was modified with three instead of four stripes.
Mike Start

On the 4th of July 1986, an eastbound Santa Fe freight with red 9522-5664-red 9539-red 8744-red 5117 (SF30C/SD45-2/SF30C/U36C/SD40-2) passes red SP SD45 #7562 at Mojave.
John L. Shine

Beginning with rebuilt SD45 #7562 SP's oscillating lights have been removed. This photo shows the 7562 with the rear plate intact and the dual sealed beam light gone. The 7563 (ahead of the 7562) shows how all of the later SD45 rear light packages were changed.
John L. Shine

At left is a rare view of Barstow's refueling rack with four merger painted units on the point on September 9, 1986. The units are (from left) 5358-7208-9537-7226 (SD45/SD45-2/SF30C/SD45-2). One of Santa Fe's hottest, the 1-188-09 train (below) speeds through Amboy in the California desert with red 7216-5078-5426-5430 (SD45-2/SD40-2/2 SD45's) on September 10, 1986. Since the ICC denial, the 7216 has been renumbered 5816.
Both Mike Martin/SFSP Corp.

Paul Lukens

This is perhaps the last rail photograph taken in 1985. Late in the evening of Dec. 31st, SP's pair of passenger SDP45's, red 3207 and 3201 along with a pair of Amtrak F40PH's, arrive at LA with a holiday packed "Coast Starlight". Just east of Mojave on February 23, 1986 (right), five cowl units bring the 1-179-21 train toward the junction with the SP for the climb over the Tehachapis. All but one SDFP45, and many SDF45's, were painted in the merger red and yellow scheme.

Mike Martin

This photo of the 843 train, just east of Sullivan's Curve, in Cajon Pass on May 3, 1986, illustrates the difference in the location of the nose stripe on Santa Fe's cowl units. Notice how the nose stripe on SD45 #5346 lines up with the cab numbers, however, the stripe is much lower on SDF45 #5975 due to the location of the nose lights.

Joe Shine

Southern Pacific SD40T-2 "snoot" #8377, is in command of this Roseville-West Colton freight at Canyon in Cajon Pass. Three SP "SD40T-2 snoots" had been painted in the red and yellow scheme; 8315, 8351 and 8377. *John L. Shine*

A check of the Sacramento Locomotive Works in February 1986 (below), finds several recently shopped units waiting for parts. Gray and red SD45 #7492 and SD45T-2 #9352 flank rebuilt SD45's 7563, 7561 and (behind the 9352) 7562. The 7562 and 7563 have had their top mounted oscillating lights removed and are waiting for Santa Fe style roof mounted rotating beacons. *Joe Shine*

20

On a cool crisp morning of January 4, 1986, Santa Fe's hot 893 train has just crested Cajon Summit powered by three newly rebuilt SD39's, 1562, 1566 and 1564, followed by two more rather drab blue and yellow units. During this period Santa Fe was rebuilding their two major wash racks at Argentine and Barstow, with the result that many units became very grimy. *Bob Hanggie*

A tremendous amount of motive power is required to move the "Oil Train" from Bakersfield to Sylmar, where the helpers are currently cut out. This train, on July 5, 1986, led by red SD40T-2 #8526, requires 16,200hp up front (5 units), and a 18,000hp mid-train helper set (6 units).
David Giglio

Diesel locomotives were not the only rolling stock painted in anticipation of the merger. The first caboose to receive a test scheme was class Ce-1 #999088 at Topeka on April 25, 1986. Originally lettered "SPSF 999088", the middle "PS" was covered when brought out into public view. The hack was later repainted and lettered like the Ce-2 below.
Thomas A. Chenoweth

Class Ce-2 caboose 999528 illustrates the bright red with yellow ends and lettering adopted for the crummies. Very few Santa Fe, and only one Southern Pacific, caboose received the "new image" paint and lettering scheme.
Thomas A. Chenoweth

The lone Southern Pacific bay-window caboose to receive the bright red and yellow scheme is SP 4726 from class C-50-9, photographed arriving at West Colton from Los Angeles on November 18, 1986.
Mike Start

Extended vision caboose 999700 from class Ce-8 also received a new coat of paint. One variation is noted on this cab, as opposed to the Ce-2, is that everything on the ends, except the brake rigging, is yellow including the steps.
Thomas A. Chenoweth

In this photo many variations of the merger paint scheme can be seen. The SW1500 has a red cab with Santa Fe style numbers and small "SP" initals, while high hood GP9 #3735's yellow cab has the larger, now obsolete, Espee type numbers.

Mark A. Denis

Santa Fe red GP35 #3592, ex-2835, was renumbered during June 1986 in a complicated renumbering program designed to open the 3000 series for newly remanufactured GP39-2's. The new number was added and the classification lights were plated over after the 2835 had been painted in the merger scheme. The 3592, with black cab numbers, was photographed at Walong on July 3, 1986.

Don Steen

Blue and yellow GP35 #3585, ex-2828, was not painted in the merger scheme, but it was renumbered, as the 3592 above. This renumbering included red number boards with white numerals, which presented a rather odd appearance. Due to the ICC's negative decision all of the 3561 class GP35's have been re-renumbered back to the 2800 series.

Mike Martin

Renumbered GP39-2 #3140 and GP35 #3585 (above) were both photographed at San Bernardino in September and August 1986, respectively. The non-rebuilt 3600 class GP39-2's received 3100 series numbers during June and July, while the newly remanufactured GP39-2's were to become the 3000 series. Since the ICC decision, the 3100's were re-renumbered back to their original 3600 class, and the rebuilds are becoming Santa Fe's 3400 class in blue/yellow.

Jerry Shine

CHANGES AFTER 7/24/86

With the ICC disapproval announcement of July 24, 1986, both roads began painting all shopped and rebuilt locomotives in their pre-merger colors.

Santa Fe's next rebuilt SD45-2 emerged from the shops in blue and yellow. It was to have been numbered 7230, instead it was outshopped as AT&SF 5830, the number series that would have been assigned to the rebuilt SD45-2's if the merger had not been in the works. The 7205, which had been slightly damaged in an accident, was in the San Bernardino Shops when the ICC made their decision. It was outshopped during the last week of August as the 5805 in the blue and yellow scheme, the first red unit to be repainted back into blue. Since then, at least a few red units have been painted back to blue and yellow, including GP40X #3803.

During August, Santa Fe's new 3100 class GP39-2's were renumbered back into the 3600 series, and the 3561 class GP35's were receiving their 2800 series numbers once again. The Cleburne rebuilt GP39-2's were outshopped in Santa Fe's 3400 series instead of the SPSF 3000 class.

Meanwhile, at Sacramento, Southern Pacific began painting their rebuilt and repaired units into their familiar gray and red scheme. Espee's SD45T-2 #6771 was the first rebuilt unit to be outshopped in gray and red from the Sacramento Locomotive Works. Unlike Santa Fe, the Southern Pacific has not yet reverted to strictly SP numbers for their rebuilt SD45T-2's.

At left is a contemporary scene of motive power at San Bernardino with merger painted SF30C's 9515 and 9550, and newly rebuilt SD45-2 #5838 in blue on October 12, 1986. Below, on July 26th, two days after the ICC decision, a stalled SP eastbound is helped at Walong by Santa Fe 5060 taken from the 991 train.

Jerry Shine

Mark A. Denis

On June 26, 1986, the eastbound harbor train (LA harbor-Barstow) is assigned a very colorful consist; 7222-5960-7219-7221 (SD45-2/SDF45/2 SD45-2's). The last two had been lettered with the complete "SPSF" while in San Bernardino.
Mike Start

Since the ICC's negative decision of July 24, 1986, Santa Fe and Southern Pacific have both reverted to painting rebuilt and shopped units in their respective (pre-merger) schemes. Recently remanufactured Santa Fe SD45-2 #5834 (above right) and Southern Pacific SD45T-2 #6771 (right) are the 6-axle units now going through the upgrading process at San Bernardino and Sacramento respectively, while Cleburne is gearing up for the GP39-2 rebuild program.
Both Jerry Shine

MERGER PAINTED LOCOMOTIVES

NEW PAINT - SANTA FE NUMBERS - "SF" INITIALS

- **SLUGS=** 109 123 127 129 140(2nd) 142 143 144 145(2nd) 146(2nd)
- **GP7=** 1316 1327 2001 2064 2126 2138
- **GP9=** 2250 2291
- **GP20=** 3012 3018 3019 3028 3029 3031 3048 3052 3056 3058 3063 3068 3070 3072 3073 3074
- **GP30=** 2703 2705 2714 2717 2718 2720 2724 2733 2734 2735 2736 2737 2745 2748 2750 2752 2753 2755 2759 2764 2768 2770 2772 2773 2775 2776 2780
- **GP35=** 2814 2835=(3592 Blk cab no's) 2837=(3594 blk no boards) 2842 2848 2858 2867 2879 2923 2932 2935 2946 2959
- **GP38=** 2312
- **GP38-2=** 2370 2371 2372 2373 2374 2375
- **GP39-2=** 3600=(3100) 3613=(3113) 3632=(3132) 3669 3676 3679=(3177) 3683=(3181) 3693=(3190) 3696
- **GP40X=** 3803 3805
- **GP50=** 3828
- **SD39=** 1562 1564 1566 1568 1569 1570 1571 1572 1573 1574 1575 (1569 orig. ptd. blue in shop only)
- **SD40-2=** 5022 5023 5026 5060 5062 5068 5077 5082 5093 5098 5107 5117 5132 5159 5161 5182 5184 5192
- **SD45=** 5302 5331 5333 5335 5337 5338 5339 5342 5344 5345 5346 5347 5348 5349 5350 5351 5352 5353 5354 5355 5357 5358 5359 5360 5362=(blk no boards) 5364 (5394 wht & yel "SF") 5401 5402
- **SD45-2=** 5676 5679 5682 5694 5699 5709
- **SD45-2u=** 7200 7201 7202 7203 7204 7205 7206 7207 7208 7209 7210 7211 7212 7213 7214 7215 7216 7217 7218 7219 7220 7221 7222 7223 7224 7225 7226 7227 7228 7229=(5800-5804, 5806-5829)
- **SDF45=** 5950 5953 5954 5955 5957 5959 5960 5963 5964 5966 5968 5969 5970 5973 5975 5976 5977 5980 5986 5987 5989
- **SDFP45=** 5990 5991 5992 5993 5996 5997 5998
- **B23-7=** 6354 6365 6373 6374 6375 6378 6380 6388 6396 6404
- **B36-7=** 7486 7497
- **U36C=** 8736 8739 8741 8744 8746 8749 8750 8752 8753 8755
- **C30-7=** 8013 8016 8018 8019 8032 8051 8055 8056 8061 8063 8066 8068 8069 8070 8072 8073 8075 8076 8077 8078 8079 8080 8081 8085 8086 8087 8088 8089 8090 8104 8105 8133 8139 8141 8142 8146 8148 8150 8154 8155 8156 8158 8159 8162 8164 8165
- **SF30-C=** 9510-9553

NEW PAINT - SOUTHERN PACIFIC NUMBERS - "SP" INITIALS

- **SW900E=** 1192
- **SW1500=** 2527 2539 2575
- **MP15=** 2700
- **GP9E=** 2873 3370 3735 3739 3775 3778 3784 3792 3846
- **GP35E=** 6304 6322 6354 6356 6361
- **GP35=** 6533 6566 6577 6606 6619 6640 6644
- **GP40-2=** 7672
- **SD9E=** 4327 4345 4347 4354 4363 4372 4375 4377 (4381 sold) 4418 4420
- **SD35E=** 2968
- **SD40R=** 7303 7310 7319 7357 7361 7384
- **SD40T-2=** 8286 8315 8351 8377 8521 8526 8530 8573
- **SD45=** 9092 9098
- **SD45R=** 7399 7420 7430 7443 7457 7514 (7551 wht & yel "SP") 7556 7557 7558 7559 7560 7561 7562 7563 7564 7565 7566
- **SDP45=** 3201 3207 3208
- **SD45T-2=** 9182 9192 9207 9208 9229 9303 9318 9319 9331 9338 9346 9350 9351 9362
- **SD45T-2R=** 9500=(6767) 9501=(6768) 6769 6770
- **B30-7=** 7859 7874

This is not an official list, but one derived from many sources. There was not an official record compiled by either railroad, and this list is believed to be at least 98% complete.

ATSF POOL POWER / RUN THROUGHS

Prior to April 1984 it was very unusual to find pool or run-through power operating on Santa Fe's Coast Lines. However in April, with the signing of a run-through pact with the Burlington Northern, Santa Fe on the BN and vice versa, has become rather commonplace. On October 12, 1986, Santa Fe SD45-2 #5626 followed by BN 7163-2601-7834 (SD40-2/GP38-2B/SD40-2) leads the 868 train up Cajon Pass.
Both Jerry Shine

Santa Fe merger painted C30-7 #8051 (right) along with SD40-2 #5028 and BN SD40-2 #6840 head east from San Bernardino with the 843 train on October 3, 1986. Bound for the Powder River Basin with empty UFIX coalhoppers (below), five SD40-2's, BN 7831-ATSF 5084-5067-BN B unit 7500-ATSF 5070 head down Crawford Hill, Nebraska in May 1985. *Below Joe Shine*

27

One of the more interesting locations to catch mixed power is on the Joint Line between Denver and Pueblo, Colorado. Heading toward Denver, on Rio Grande track, is such a consist with an empty UFIX unit coal train powered by ATSF red 8055-red 8088-5065- BN 5061-5590 (2 C30-7's/SD40-2/2 C30-7's).

Mike Start

Heading north from Guernsey, Wyoming on BN track with a OGEX (Oklahoma Gas and Electric) unit coal train is BN 7194-5831-ATSF 8124-BN 5032-5081 (SD40-2/U30C/3 C30-7's) on June 2, 1985. This train is returning to the Powder River Basin from the utility plant at Red Rock, Oklahoma which is located on Santa Fe trackage.

Joe Shine

During July 1986, the Kansas City Southern gave the Santa Fe four GP40's in return for horsepower hours owed. The 885 train (Los Angeles–Texas) heads east on July 11, 1986 with merger renumbered GP35 #3563–2882–KCS 755–750–ATSF 2727–red 2720 (2 GP35's/2 GP40's/2 GP 30's). *Mike Start*

Entering Abo Canyon, New Mexico, late in the evening of May 22, 1986, is a very colorful consist led by ATSF red 9538–red 5161–BN 6757–7135–8027 (SF30C/4 SD40-2's). The Burlington Northern units are returning east after bringing the 698 train (BN–Santa Fe run–through) to Barstow. *Steve Dunham*

Santa Fe U36C's, 8748 and 8775, lead Conrail GP38-2's, 7985 and 8062, at Helendale west of Barstow, in November 1984. CR units run through to the Santa Fe via the Streator connection, but are normally turned at Kansas City. *Joe Shine*

UP 3713–ATSF 5055–5020–UP 3716 prepare to head east after dropping the Bandini Turn at Rivera, California. This power is from a joint unit coal train which originates on the Union Pacific and terminates at the St. Joseph power plant in Arizona. While the coal is being unloaded, Santa Fe uses the power in their general freight pool out of Barstow. *Joe Shine*

On February 16, 1985 Amtrak's "Southwest Limited" arrived in Los Angeles with Santa Fe U36C #8744 and Amtrak F40PH #285 as the motive power. Obviously, the lead F40PH had developed a problem on the eastern end of the system and the big GE filled in. The following day a westbound freight was photographed at Ash Hill, between Needles and Barstow, with F40PH #254 now running, in the freight consist. *John L. Shine*

SP POOL POWER/RUN THROUGHS

Union Pacific motive power working on the Southern Pacific has been common for many years, and solid UP sets on the point have been noted from time to time. An eastbound freight, in full dynamics, holds tonnage at bay with SP 8248–UP 3103–3161–3515 (SD40T–2/3 SD40–2's) approaching Canyon, in Cajon Pass.
Joe Shine

With the expiration of a joint coal hauling contract with the Santa Fe, SP's 8489–8498 series SD40T–2's have returned to home rails. On October 3, 1986, SP 8495–8498–Milw 170–SP 8491–8489 leave West Colton with a Soo Line run through train. (Milwaukee Road is now owned by Soo Line.) *Jerry Shine*

On May 30, 1985, the SOHOI (Southern Ry.–Houston Interchange) heads through New Iberia, La. enroute to Englewood (Houston) with SP 7402–7408–Sou 7082 (2 SD45's/ GP50). The Southern Ry. and Southern Pacific routinely run through New Orleans on each others railroad. *Paul Lukens*

Repayment of horsepower hours owed is rather commonplace between railroads, and on April 19, 1986 a pair of Southern Pacific SD40's, red 7310 and 7341 are repaying the Santa Fe. At Barstow, a red Santa Fe B36-7 #7497 leads an eastbound "pig train". To photograph a Santa Fe red, SP red, SP gray and Santa Fe blue in the same consist is extremely rare. *Mike Lepker*

At Canyon, in Cajon Pass on May 10, 1986, a westbound Southern Pacific drag freight contains motive power from three railroads, making for a very interesting consist. On the point is SP 7316-9042-D&RGW 3129-SP 8250-UP 3410 (SD40/SD45/GP40-2/SD40T-2/SD40-2). *John L. Shine*

Loma Linda, just east of Colton, is the location eastbound trains pick up helpers for the climb to Beaumont. A freight, powered by Rio Grande GP40's, waits on the main, as a helper set headed by SP 7430, a red rebuilt SD45, will be added on the point.
Frank Keller

Southern Pacific gained a short cut from the Northwest to Kansas City and St. Louis when the Rio Grande was granted trackage rights over the MoPac east of Pueblo, Colorado. Rio Grande's Tennessee Pass acts as a "bridge line" between the SP at Ogden, Utah, and the Midwest, thus SP and D&RGW power are freely mixed. Such a train works through Mitchell, Colorado, on the Grande with D&RGW 5342-5393-SP 9332-7371-7510 on May 22, 1986.
John L. Shine

The gyralight has been turned on, the crew from Salt Lake City has departed, and the new crew from Helper, Utah is ready to head this eastbound freight, with three Rio Grande and three Southern Pacific units, toward Grand Junction, where the train will head for Tennessee Pass in May 1985.
Joe Shine

During the spring of 1986, a power short Southern Pacific borrowed units from several railroads including the Illinois Central Gulf. Most of the units were kept on the eastern end of the system but a few strayed west. On March 14, 1986, the eastbound LACHT prepares to leave Industry, California with SP 7242-8564-red 7556-ICG 2540-SP 7546 (GP40-2/SD40T-2/SD45/GP35 on Alco trucks/SD45).
Mike Start

Two more units that showed up in the west were IC GP40 #3018, complete with the diamond herald, and GM&O 620, a GP35 with Alco trucks, photographed at West Colton on April 26, 1986. *John L. Shine*

Repaying the power which Southern Pacific borrowed a couple of months earlier, Illinois Central Gulf 8017-7742-SP 7504 (GP10/GP8/SD45) head the CR5 (Chicago-Baton Rouge) train through Effingham, Illinois, on July 24, 1986.
John L. Shine

On May 23, 1986, an eastbound Union Pacific unit coal train leaves Cheyenne, Wyoming with a mixture of motive power consisting of UP 2918-2496-3403-SP 7521-8334 (U30C/C30-7/SD40-2/SD45/SD40T-2). Southern Pacific and Union Pacific power operating together has probably been the most common pooled power for many years. *John L. Shine*

An eastbound Southern Pacific freight (right), led by UP SD40-2 #3557, is passing over itself at Walong (Tehachapi Loop). *James R. Doughty*

Below, a UP eastbound running on Santa Fe track, at Blue Cut in Cajon Pass, has motive power from UP, C&NW and SP. On occasion SP power is returned at LA, but usually operates back to Ogden before returning to home rails. *Joe Shine*

Burlington Northern units enter and leave the Espee system through Kansas City and Portland. On November 21, 1985, SP 7427-7635-BN 6928-7500-7142-7140-4067 (SD45/GP40-2/SD40-2/SD40-2B/2 SD40-2's/B30-7B) bring the NOOAT (New Orleans-Oakland/Trailers) into old Colton for a crew change. The BN power had worked the KCTUG (Kansas City-Tucson/Grain) to Tucson, then the power worked back to El Paso where they picked up the NOOAT, and headed toward Portland, their final destination on the SP. *John L. Shine*

John L. Shine

On December 16, 1984 the KCLAT (above) is waiting at old Colton for a clear block at West Colton Interlocking (Santa Fe crossing) with DRGW 5364-BN 3054-DRGW 5332-SSW 9391-SP 9316 (SD40T-2/GP40-2/SD40T-2/2 SD45T-2's). While it is not unusual for Rio Grande units to lead an SP train, it is rarely mixed with other pool power. On December 22, 1984 (below) a westbound freight waits at Loma Linda while the rear helpers are cut out. At this late date it was very unusual to find BN F45's in pool service. *Joe Shine*

The marquis in the front of Electro-Motive Division's Los Angeles plant, in April 1984, tells it like it is, "Santa Fe Southern Pacific Corporation, we are pulling for you".   *Joe Shine*

LOCOMOTIVE TESTING

The two major locomotive builders in the United States, Electro Motive Division and General Electric, both have sales staffs to entice railroads to purchase their respective products. Both have entered the field of micro processor equipped locomotives within the last couple of years which makes for a much more efficient locomotive, but at the same time the price tag has been driven upwards of one million dollars per unit. This in turn has lead the railroads to rebuild or remanufacture many of their older locomotives.

In an effort to demonstrate just how good their new locomotives are, the builders arrange for test units of their own and from other railroads to be tested on a potential buyers own rails.

Three GE B39-8's (AT&SF 7400-7402) are on a long term lease for testing on the Santa Fe. Southern Pacific also tested four EMD GP50's from the Southern Railway (SOU 7052, 7054, 7073 and 7084) in March 1983, and later in September they ran tests with GE's B36-8 #606. Santa Fe conducted extensive tests with three of EMD's 6-axle SD60 demo's (EMD 1, 2 and 4) during July 1985, and EMD's 4-axle GP60's (EMD 5, 6 and 7) in May 1986.

Other roads have also tested new motive power from the Santa Fe and Southern Pacific. In December 1979 and through the early part of 1980 the Burlington Northern borrowed SP's four GP40X's for testing. Also in 1979 Conrail and Southern borrowed Santa Fe's GP40X's, and during 1981 the Illinois Central Gulf and Southern Railway both borrowed Santa Fe GP50's, and in August 1985 Santa Fe traded their three 4-axle B39-8's for three 6-axle C32-8's from Conrail.

MOTIVE POWER REQUIREMENTS

You may ask, what this all has to do with motive power? Well, almost every improvement that had been undertaken had a direct bearing on the number of diesel units that would have been required, and also just what type of units would have been needed. For an example, the more trains that could have avoided a major mountain pass meant less units that would have been required for helper service. On the other hand, the more traffic that could have been generated by faster schedules would have meant more diesel units that would be needed.

Both roads have found that high horsepower four-axle units can best expedite the hot piggyback traffic which constitutes much of the east-west business of today. Most recently Southern Pacific has opted for EMD GP40-2's and GE B36-7's, while Santa Fe has gone with GP50's from EMD and B36-7's from GE. Therefore it was believed to be very possible that the initial motive power purchases made by the new SPSF would most likely have been GP60's from EMD and/or B39-8's from GE. Santa Fe usually split their orders and it is believed that would have been the course taken.

After making several test runs across the Santa Fe system, SD60's EMD 1-4-ATSF 5382 bring the 358 train into Amarillo, Texas on a rainy July 16, 1985. The 5382 is filling in for EMD 2, which had been returned to EMD for repairs.
John L. Shine

Electro-Motive Division tests many of their new, high-tech locomotives on Santa Fe's Raton Pass, between Colorado and New Mexico. In July 1984, EMD's test train uses brand new Seaboard System SD50's, 8525 and 8526, for wheel slip and traction tests.
Mike Start

During the spring of 1986, EMD's GP60's barnstormed the west. On April 25, 1986, GP60's EMD 5, 6 and 7 are in charge of the 1-199-23 train near Mojave, California, with Santa Fe business cars "Mountainair" and "Santa Fe" on the rear. The set of power and business cars returned on the 1-991-26 train the following day.
Mike Martin/SFSP Corp.

Santa Fe's Public Relations Department, not missing a chance for publicity, has added white flags with the Santa Fe logo to EMD SD60 demonstrators. Here EMD 1, leads Santa Fe's 881 train east near Riverside, California, on July 13, 1985.
Joe Shine

EMD GP60's 7, 6 and 5, along with a SP SD45, work east through San Timoteo Canyon, on a SP eastbound freight in October 1986. With the elaborate light packages, the GP60's appear to have been built for the Southern Pacific. The GP60's are equipped with a new type of nose and cab front with more curved edges thought to help cut down on wind resistance.
Bob Gallegos

General Electric's B39-8's are on the Santa Fe by virtue of a long-term lease. These three microprocessor equipped units have been tested on a number of foreign roads since being leased by the Santa Fe. As this book is being assembled, they are on the Burlington Northern.
Joe Shine

During the summer of 1985, some of General Electric's third generation locomotives showed up in unusual places. Santa Fe's three B39-8's, 7400-7402, were traded to Conrail for three of their C32-8's. These big 6-axle GE's worked extensively in Texas, and on Santa Fe's Duval unit sulphur train, as seen here, with a few cars of general freight on the front, heading down the Carlsbad Branch, west of Clovis, New Mexico, on August 20, 1985.
Don Steen

ICC DECISION 7/24/86

The Santa Fe Southern Pacific Corporation had issued their "Merger Update No. 13" to notify their employees that the Interstate Commerce Commision would render their decision on July 24, 1986. It was widely thought that the merger would be granted and that after several appeals from some of the roads which had contested the merger were heard, the machinery which had been set up for post merger operations would be implemented.

All parties involved were in Washington D.C. on July 24th to hear the ICC decision. Many of the railroad officials from the corporation sat in stunned silence as the commissioners rendered their 4-1 vote disapproving the merger of the two rail lines.

Chairman John Schmidt said the decision was "a horrible mistake" and that "we (the corporation) will have to sell something." He was referring to the fact that ICC stated that the SFSP Corporation would have to spin off either one or both of the railroads. Later at a news conference he stated that shippers in the West and Southwest would be harmed by the rejection. He also said, "This is not doomsday" and that "there are many things we can do with one or both of the railroads", and stated, "we will regroup".

Several days later it was announced that the corporation would appeal the decision.

One of the interesting aspects of the decision was that the commission's staff recommended approving the merger, but four of the five commissioners stated the adverse effect on competition in some parts of the country outweighed public benefits. This was very interesting considering some of the mergers that have already taken place, which had helped weaken both the Southern Pacific and Santa Fe in the first place, and also considering the weak financial position of the Espee in particular.

During late August the SFSP Corporation asked the ICC to delay issuing its written decision rejecting the proposed merger, and petitioned the ICC to reconsider its merger rejection. In early October, the ICC said that it would deny the company's request and would render its written decision later that month. At the same time the ICC gave the corporation 60 days to prepare a petition asking them to reconsider their decision.

Meanwhile, the corporation held negotiations with the Denver & Rio Grande and Union Pacific in order to reach an accord with the two roads. If the merger is approved by the ICC, trackage rights and lease agreements would be implemented which would alleviate competitive concerns by the ICC.

The corporation will be submitting new evidence and requests from shippers, other railroads and employees to reopen merger hearings and reverse their decision.

Even other railroads voiced their concern. Picture, if you will, the entire railroad network as a large chain, with one of the links (roads) being weak. That chain is only as strong as the weakest link. All of the railroads know this, and need to be concerned.

A "Rail-O-Gram" calling on U.S. Senators and Representatives to support the Santa Fe and Southern Pacific merger was signed by thousands of people attending Railroad Days at Topeka, Kansas. The 50-foot, 70-ton car was painted yellow and black to represent a telegram. I didn't forget the modelers in our midst. The car, ATSF 524045, is an insulated box car from class Bx-159 (reclassified from RR-81), built in March 1963. As a Bx-159, it was painted bright red, with "Super Shock Control - A smoother ride" lettering. It is pictured here on August 28, 1986, prior to the Railroad Days signing.   *Thomas A. Chenoweth*

Both of the MP15AC/slug sets assigned to Tucson sit idle in the afternoon sun on August 12, 1984. The 2734/1013 and 2733/1012 have spent most of their careers in this Arizona yard, meanwhile the 2732/1010 and 2735/1011 were assigned to Roseville in northern California.
James R. Doughty

MP15AC's 2732 and 2735 along with slugs 1010 and 1011 have spent most of their years switching the Eugene, Oregon and Roseville, California yards. There were only four SP 4-axle yard slugs, which were all built by GE from retired L&N EMD switchers.
Vic Reyna collection

Santa Fe's two small yard slugs, 120 and 121, have always been assigned to Chicago's Corwith Yard since they were converted from NW2's at Cleburne Shops in 1973. They have been mated with rebuilt GP7's 1310 and 1311, both of which still have their original round roofs.
John L. Shine

SLUGS

There are really only two major types of slugs on the system, yard slugs and road slugs. The Southern Pacific refers to their slugs as TEBU's (Tractive Effort Booster Units), and that best defines their operation. They are actually locomotives with traction motors but without prime movers, and receive electrical current to operate these traction motors from a locomotive with special connections called a "mother", or control unit. They operate at slow speed exerting great starting tractive effort making them ideal for heavy yard drags, and on the road where tonnage is a factor rather than speed. A slug can be operated with any mother unit, and are sometimes traded around during the shopping of either of the units. However, the four motor slugs are usually kept with the four axle mother units, and the six motor slugs usually operate with the six axle mothers.

**SOUTHERN PACIFIC/4 AXLE YARD SP 1010-1013
(SPSF 100-103)**

In 1979 SP contracted with the General Electric Apparatus Shops at Minneapolis to construct four yard slugs to be operated with four MP15AC mothers which had been purchased in October 1975. The slugs, SP 1010-1013, were built from retired L&N EMD switchers between June and August 1979. After being mated with MP15AC's 2732-2735, they have since worked Eugene, Roseville, Taylor (LA), and Tucson yards.

**SANTA FE/4 AXLE YARD   ATSF 120-121
(SPSF 104-105)**

Santa Fe's first two B-B yard slugs, 120 and 121, were converted from a pair of retired EMD NW2 switchers at the Cleburne Shops in April and July 1973. They have always been assigned to Corwith Yard in Chicago where they work with GP7 mother units.

**ATSF 123-125, 116-119 & 115
(SPSF 106-112 & 116)**

Eight additional slugs were constructed by Santa Fe's Cleburne Shops for yard service from retired and secondhand EMD first generation road units. These included five UP Geeps purchased through a junk dealer, a pair of Santa Fe retired GP7's, and a F7B. They were all built between October 1978 and October 1981, and were numbered 115-119 and 123-125. A few of the 115 class originally worked with SD26 mothers (now retired), but now all are commonly found working with 1310 class GP7 mothers.

**SANTA FE/4 AXLE ROAD/YARD   ATSF 101-109
(SPSF 113-115 & 117-122)**

Potash is mined in the Carlsbad, New Mexico area, and heavy slow drags are the order of the day. In 1972 Santa Fe mated 14 CF7's with a like number of road slugs rebuilt from F3 and F7 B-units. As the years of strenuous service began to catch up with these units a replacement program was initiated in 1981, and nine new slugs were rebuilt at Cleburne before a decision was made not to employ their use at Carlsbad, and the program was terminated. Slugs 101(2nd)-109(2nd) were then mated with 1310 class GP7's and are currently assigned to yard service. Slugs 115-119 and 123-125 are operationally identical.

**SANTA FE/6 AXLE YARD   ATSF 140-146
(SPSF 150-156)**

The original slugs 140 (from ex-Alco RSD5), 145 and 146 (from ex-Alco RSD15's), which had been assigned to Barstow were retired in 1985.

Santa Fe GP7 #1329 and slug 108 handle the switching chores at Wichita, Kansas on July 22, 1986. The 108 was constructed from a retired Conrail GP7 at Cleburne in 1983. It was originally intended to be a road slug out of Carlsbad, New Mexico. *John L. Shine*

SLUGS CONTINUED

Slug 123, the only yard slug constructed from a F7B unit, worked the Barstow Yard during its first few years of service. It and a SD26 handled much of the switching at the east end, while the CRSD20's mated with 6-axle slugs worked the hump. The 123, now mated with a 1310 class GP7, currently works on the Eastern and Western Lines.
Mark A. Denis

Santa Fe slug 116, here mated with rebuilt GP7 1314, works at Brownwood, Texas on August 19, 1985. Note the standard GP9 frame as compared with the fabricated frame on slug 123 (above), which was constructed from a F7B unit. *Don Steen*

The San Bernardino Shops swapped Chrome Locomotive Works the three retired slugs for three retired locomotive hulks to be rebuilt into new slugs for Barstow's hump yard which were mated with newly rebuilt SD39 (1556 class) mother units. The newly constructed slugs 140(2nd) and 145-146(2nd) were constructed from ex-NW 2964 nee IT 2304 SD39; ex-SP 5303 SD39; and ex-SP 6917 SD35. Slugs #141-144 (ex-Alco RSD5's) are still assigned to Argentine (Kansas City) and are now working with rebuilt SD39's of the 1556-1575 series.

ATSF 126-129
(SPSF 157-160)

A pair of C-C yard slugs, 128 and 129, were constructed at Cleburne from retired UP SD24B units purchased secondhand from scrap dealers for that purpose, and were outshopped in August and October 1979. Likewise two more, 127 and 126, were outshopped in October 1980 and May 1981 respectively, and all four were assigned to Argentine for hump service.

Newly painted hump slugs (from left) 143, 142 and 144 bask in the sun at Argentine, Kansas on July 23, 1986, waiting to be mated with recent San Bernardino Shop rebuilt SD39's (1556 class), which now have hump slug controls. Three of the six-axle slugs rebuilt from Alco products, 140, 145 and 146 have already been retired at San Bernardino and replaced with new slugs rebuilt from EMD SD's. *John L. Shine*

SLUGS CONTINUED

Santa Fe recently remanufactured SD39's idle between shifts at Bartstow where they have been assigned since being rebuilt as slug mothers in 1985. Red #1575 is mated with red hump slug 140 and blue 1556 is mated with red slug 145. This pair is Santa Fe's highest and lowest numbered SD39's.

Frank Keller

Hump slug #129, converted from a Union Pacific SD24B in October 1979, has since been working in Argentine, Kansas. These six-axle EMD slugs had previously been mated with EMD SD24's, then SD26's, and are now mated with rebuilt SD39's. Since this photo was taken in 1983, the 129 has been painted in the merger red and yellow.

Brand new slug #145 pauses at Fullerton, California, and is enroute back to San Bernardino to be mated with a SD39 slug mother after being weighed at LA's Hobart Yard. The new 140, 145 and 146 are easily distinguished from the 126-129 series by only four brake cylinders per truck and the former have large fuel tanks.

Mark A. Denis

Freshly outshopped hump slug #140 has just been mated on the point of brand new slug mother #1575 at San Bernardino for testing, just prior to being sent to their new home at Barstow in California's high desert. The three new slugs, 140, 145 and 146, are all painted in merger paint, and normally work behind the SD39.

John L. Shine

Since many of the SD39's and some of the slugs have been painted in merger colors many variations can be found. On September 13, 1986, red SD39 1562 is mated with blue 4-axle slug #125, while in the background blue SD39 #1557 is mated with blue 6-axle slug (ex-UP SD24B) #126.   *John L. Shine*

Joe Shine

45

Every once-in-a-while a photographer finds himself in the right place at the right time. On July 3, 1986, Don Steen photographed SP 7952-1605-7941 and a tunnel motor working through Walong (Tehachapi Loop) with a long heavy drag freight. This definitely is not a normal location to find TEBU sets, and it is believed that the set was being transferred from northern California to the southeast.

SOUTHERN PACIFIC/4 AXLE ROAD SP 1600-1613 (SPSF 200-213)

Not many railroads have operated road slugs, but the Santa Fe had been using old F3 and F7 B units converted to road slugs around Carlsbad, N.M. on potash operations since 1972. They have since been retired, but in 1980 when the Southern Pacific took delivery of their prototype #1600 from Morrison-Knudsen both roads operated road slugs in the Arizona and New Mexico area. SP followed that initial TEBU (Tractive Effort Booster Unit) with thirteen more constructed from retired GE U25B's at their own Sacramento Shops between April 1981 and May 1982.

The TEBU's operate with EMD GP40-2's in the SP 7940-7959 series and rebuilt (in 1982) GP40's in the SSW 7960-7967 series. They usually call Eugene, Tucson and Houston home, and operate on slow (less than 30mph) drag freights on branch lines.

Morrison-Knudsen constructed SP's original TEBU, #1600, from a retired UP U25B. The only visible difference from the SP built units is the air cylinder just above the fuel tank only on the right side. This set is working through Shaz, Arizona on October 20, 1980.

Mark A. Denis

THE SWITCHERS

SANTA FE	ATSF 1453
SW900	(SPSF 300)

Constructed in July 1937, Electro-Motive Corporation (EMC) model SC, AT&SF #2153 was the last of four units in the 2150 class. The 600hp unit was assigned as a passenger switcher and equipped with a steam generator which had been removed from Santa Fe's first passenger diesel #1L in Febuary 1939. The experiment was short lived, as the steam equipment was removed in October 1940.

The four switchers were renumbered 650-653 in early 1953, and returned to EMD four years later for rebuilding. The units outshopped by La Grange were almost completely new SW900's rated at 900hp. They retained their 650 series numbers.

The 653 was assigned to local switching around Atchison, Kansas for many years. It was renumbered 1153 in August 1974, and was renumbered again to 1453 in January 1977.

SOUTHERN PACIFIC	SP 1191-1199
SW900E	(SPSF 301-309)

Southern Pacific took delivery of a pair of EMD SW900's, SP 4624 and 4625, in April 1954, followed by a second order for eight more, SP 4626-4633, in June. Their prime mover is EMD's 12-cylinder 567C engine rated at 900hp. These orange and black tiger striped units were equipped with multiple-unit controls, and large Mars signal lights. They were originally assigned to Oakland and Los Angeles, but all were soon gathered in the south for local branch line service on the light rail of SP's subsidiary, Pacific Electric.

Changes came after 1958 when gray and red became the vogue, and in 1965 when the ten units were renumbered SP 1170-1179.

After more than twenty years of service the SW900's entered Houston Shops for upgrading and emerged between July and December 1974, as SW900E's SP 1190-1199. They were returned to the west and have been working in northern California ever since.

Santa Fe leans toward converting first generation diesels, such as F7's (CF7's), GP7's and GP9's, into switchers rather than buy new switching units. Nearly all of their switchers have been retired during the last few years with the exception of EMD SW900 #1453. It currently works the Arkansas City area, and is only one of a small breed of Santa Fe locomotives without the yellow warbonnet paint scheme.
Ed Chapman

Southern Pacific's shop switcher at the Sacramento Locomotive Works, EMD SW900E #1192, has the distinction of being the first switcher to receive the merger paint scheme. If the SF would have been applied there would not have been much red left, and smaller initials were later adopted for switchers.
The 1190 was retired in 1979, but the remaining nine were still on the roster in 1986, however most have been stored.
Shirley Burman Steinheimer

SWITCHERS CONTINUED

SOUTHERN PACIFIC   SP 1307-1337*
NW2E   (SPSF 310-317)

Although Espee owned ten prewar EMD 1000hp NW2's, and Cotton Belt purchased four in 1949, none of these switchers were considered for upgrading.

The NW2's that were to become NW2E's were all purchased by the Southern Pacific in 1949. These orange and black tiger striped switchers were originally numbered in two different groups. Twenty-three units, were ordered for the Pacific Lines (west of El Paso), and were numbered SP 1403-1425, while seventeen went to the Texas & New Orleans as T&NO 72-88. During the 1965 general renumbering program they were numbered SP 1931-1953 and 1914-1930 respectively. After the renumbering there were still many NW2's working on the Texas Lines adorned in the then obsolete orange and black scheme.

The 1930 and 1948 were retired in 1968 and 1969 respectively, while the remaining thirty-eight NW2's were ready for upgrading.

Beginning in March 1971, they entered the GRIP program at the Houston, Texas Shops and emerged as NW2E's #1300-1337. The rebuilding of the NW2's was completed in October of 1972, and most have stayed in Texas and Louisiana, with a few assigned to the San Francisco bay area. They have been in and out of storage for many years as business dictates. The 1315 was the first rebuilt NW2 to leave the roster late in 1984 followed by the 1300, 1301, 1303 and 1330 in 1985. Fourteen more, 1305-1306, 1308-1310, 1313-1314, 1316-1319, 1328-1329 and 1335, left the roster in February 1986, and by mid-1986 there were only eight left; 1307, 1311, 1321, 1324, 1326, 1331, 1336-1337.

COTTON BELT   SSW/SP 2250-2290*
SOUTHERN PACIFIC   (SPSF 318-355)
SW1200

There were actually two distinct groups of Southern Pacific/Cotton Belt SW1200's on the roster. The early units built for the Texas & New Orleans in 1954 and 1957, which were upgraded to SW1200E's, and the newer group which were purchased by the Cotton Belt and Southern Pacific between December 1964 and April 1966.

The first group of newer SW1200's, which have never been rebuilt, were delivered to the Cotton Belt as SSW 1062-1069 in February 1964, followed by a second order which went into service between December 1964 and February 1965 as SSW 1070-1073. This second order was immediately followed by the first ten SW1200's for SP's Pacific Lines, SP 1597-1606. Seventeen more, SP 1607-1623, came to the Pacific Lines between May and November of 1965. By this time the systemwide general renumbering had begun, and all of the SW1200's purchased by both Cotton Belt and Southern Pacific during the early and mid-1960's were renumbered SSW 2250-2261 and SP 2262-2288. An additional five SW1200's came to the Cotton Belt during the early part of 1966 as SSW 2289-2293.

Many have been in and out of storage during the past several years. SP 2265, 2273 and 2279, plus the last three, SSW 2291-2293, have been leased and/or sold to private owners and/or shortlines.

COTTON BELT/SOUTHERN PACIFIC   SP 2294-2296
SW7E   (SPSF 356-358)

Electro-Motive's first offering of a 1200hp switcher was the SW7, a very popular model on many roads but not on the Espee. As a matter of fact, the only four SW7's on the whole system came to the Cotton Belt as their #1054-1057 in April 1950. SP/SSW purchased many 1200hp switchers from EMD later, but those were to be EMD's newer versions of SW9's and SW1200's.

The four SW7's were renumbered SSW 2200-2203 in 1965. SSW 2203 was retired in 1970, but the remaining three were upgraded at Houston Shops in October and November 1972 and January 1973 respectively. In keeping with system policy, all upgraded switchers were outshopped with Southern Pacific lettering, so the SW7E's were renumbered SP 2294-2296, losing all identity as Cotton Belt units.

COTTON BELT   SP 2298-2300,02,05-06,08
SOUTHERN PACIFIC   (SPSF 359-361, 367-370)
SW9E

The system's first 1200hp SW9's were ordered by the Cotton Belt in 1951, and were delivered in December 1951 and January 1952, as SSW 1058-1061. Twelve years would pass before any more switchers would be delivered to the Cotton Belt.

These four units were set up to operate in multiple, only with each other, for use on the new Pine Bluff hump which opened in 1958. Therefore they spent most of their active years working in and around Pine Bluff. In 1965 these black and orange switchers were renumbered SSW 2204-2207.

They were sent to Houston during the early 1970's, and upgraded in SP's GRIP program there in 1973, emerging as SP 2297-2300.

The only other group of SW9's came to Espee's Texas Lines in April 1953 as T&NO 108-112. These five switchers were renumbered SP 2208-2212 respectively, in 1965.

As with all of the other 1200hp switchers purchased during the early and mid-1950's, these SW9's were upgraded at Houston Shops between June 1973 and January 1974, and reentered service as SP 2301-2302, 2305-2306 and 2308 as SW9E's. The numbers were mingled between SW1200E's being upgraded during the same period.

48

SWITCHERS CONTINUED

The main distinguishing feature of EMD's NW2's is the small front radiator. When new, these switchers featured the orange and black tiger stripe paint scheme, front and rear foot boards, and single head lights, all of which have been gone for years. They worked the many branch lines in California and Texas, and now not only the switchers are being retired, but many of the branch lines are being abandonded.
Mark A. Denis

The Cotton Belt SW1200's differed from Southern Pacific's because of the lack of oscillating light packages and train indicators as on SP 2278 below. The 2251 was photographed switching at Pine Bluff, Arkansas on July 14, 1985.
John L. Shine

EMD SW9E #2299 idles at Houston's Hardy Street engine facility in September 1983, while not far away there are lines of stored NW2E's, SW7E's, SW9E's and SW1200's. *Joe Shine*

Southern Pacific SW1200 #2278 rests between the commute rushes at San Francisco's 7th Street engine terminal. The little switcher has all the extras such as multiple unit controls, complete side hand rails, oscillating headlight packages both front and rear, and train indicators just ahead of the exhaust stacks. *Mike Martin*

49

SWITCHERS CONTINUED

SOUTHERN PACIFIC   SP 2312-16,03,07,09-11
SW1200E   (SPSF 362-366,371-375)

The original group of SW1200's, T&NO 113-118, came in February 1954. They were numbered above the 1200hp SW9's, and differed only by a newer version of EMD's 567 prime mover and new D37B traction motors, outwardly they were nearly identical. A second group of SW1200's came exactly three years later as T&NO 123-128. All of these tiger striped SW1200's were classed as freight units with aluminum painted ends and multiple unit connections for operating together on local freights. Neither the Pacific Lines or the Cotton Belt owned any of these early SW1200's. T&NO 128 was retired in 1964 prior to being renumbered, and the remaining eleven units were placed in the SP 2213-2223 series in 1965.

The 1200hp SW9's and early SW1200's were upgraded at Houston Shops simultaneously during 1973 and 1974, with the rebuilt SW1200's being outshopped as SP 2303-2304, 2307 and 2309-2316.

The first SW1200E to be retired was the 2304, which was retired at Houston in February 1986.

SANTA FE   ATSF 1460
GP/BALD   (SPSF 600)

The most unique locomotive on Santa Fe's roster is an EMD re-engined Baldwin switcher #1460, which is one of a kind. The original locomotive was a standard 1000hp Baldwin VO-1000 switcher built in July 1943 as AT&SF 2220. It was rebuilt at the Cleburne Shops in December 1970 with an EMD 16-cylinder 567-BC prime mover. To house this larger 1500hp engine an EMD GP7 long hood was used. The Baldwin cab and frame were retained, but that was about all from the original switcher. The unit is equipped with MU connections and rides on Blomberg trucks.

The new unit was originally numbered 2450 in December 1970, and was renumbered 1160 in August 1974, and 1460 in January 1977. Most of its time has been spent on lease to the Port Terminal Railroad Association at Houston, Texas. It has since returned home to Cleburne, Texas where it now serves as the shop switcher.

SOUTHERN PACIFIC   SP/SSW 2450-2689*
COTTON BELT   (SPSF 601-833)
SW1500

The biggest news in the switcher locomotive market in sometime occurred in 1966 when EMD announced that their new 645 prime movers, which had been available a year earlier in road units, would be available in eight and twelve cylinder versions in their latest switchers, the SW1000 and SW1500.

While several other roads ordered SW1500's first, the Southern Pacific began in 1967, what was to be one of the largest fleets of SW1500 switchers in the country. With many of the older switchers from Alco, Baldwin, GE, Fairbanks-Morse, as well as some of the older EMD's ripe for replacement, and three of the five builders out of switcher production, the SW1500 was introduced just in time for the SP/SSW.

Southern Pacific tested and later purchased ten Alco center cab C-415's in 1966, but were not entirely satisfied with them. Alco later dropped out of the locomotive business completely leaving Electro-Motive as the sole producer of switchers.

Neither the Southern Pacific or Cotton Belt ever opted for the smaller SW1000, but they both went for the 1500hp, 12 cylinder 645E engined SW1500 in a big way. Between August 1967 and April 1973 a total of 240 units were purchased, 204 for SP and 36 for SSW.

They were equipped to operate with road units in regular freight service if needed, and featured EMD flexicoil trucks, allowing for a sixty-mile-an-hour speed, MU connections, full length hand rails and complete safety light clusters on both ends.

While a few SW1500's have been stored servicable from time to time, only SP 2455, 2463, 2509, 2529, 2541, 2643 and 2675 have been retired. None of the Cotton Belt SW1500's have been retired to date. The older SW1500's are approaching their twentieth birthday, and the time for rebuilding is close at hand.

SOUTHERN PACIFIC   SP 2690-2701
MP15   (SPSF 900-911)

In 1974, with a total of 316 switchers of 1200hp or less, plus the 240 SW1500's on the combined Southern Pacific/Cotton Belt roster, one would think that no more strictly switcher types would be needed for quite some time. Wrong! By 1974 EMD was marketing a newer version of their 1500hp switcher, the MP15. It was three feet longer than the SW1500 allowing for a longer wheel base for better weight distribution and a larger fuel capacity of 1300 gallons compared to the SW1500's 1100. Espee's dozen, 2690-2701, were delivered in December 1974 and January 1975, with all of the extras as on the SW1500's, as well as Blomberg trucks identical to those on EMD's F-units and GP9's.

SWITCHERS CONTINUED

Without a doubt the most unique diesel on Santa Fe's roster is #1460. It was originally a 2207 class Baldwin model VO1000 switcher #2220 built in June 1943. It was reengined at Cleburne, Texas, in December 1970, with a 16 cylinder 1500hp EMD 567BC prime mover, F7 Blomberg trucks and a GP7 long hood. In this new configuration it was numbered 2450 and spent many years on lease to the Port Terminal Railroad Association of Houston, Texas. The unit was renumbered 1160 in August 1974, and again in January 1977, to its current number, 1460. These two photos were taken at Cleburne on August 15, 1985, where it is currently in service as the shop switcher. At press time (October 1986) there were only three units on the Santa Fe roster in this obsolete paint scheme, i.e. without the yellow warbonnet; switchers 1453 and 1460, and SD45B 5501.

Mike Martin

Don Steen

SP 2539 was the first SW1500 painted in the merger red and yellow scheme early in 1986. It was assigned to San Francisco, where this photo was taken on July 19, 1986, for switching around the busy commute area, a highly visible location. This scheme was short lived however, as many changes were to take place before a standard scheme was obtained for the switchers. A later variation of the merger scheme is worn by SP SW1500 #2575 at Bakersfield July 17, 1986. Gone are the red nose stripes, large red SP style numbers, large initials, small "SP" initials between the number boards and yellow cab sides. The newer scheme also features an exaggerated yellow warbonnet.

Paul Lukens

Mark A. Denis

51

SWITCHERS CONTINUED

The LANOT (Los Angeles–New Orleans Trailer) pauses on June 5, 1986, at City of Industry, California to make a pick up. Todays unusual consist includes SP 7556–2464–6310, SD45/SW1500/GP35. When pressed with a shortage of motive power Espee sometimes has to recruite their SW1500's for road service. *Both John L. Shine*

A pair of Cotton Belt SW1500's (identical to Southern Pacific's) work the hump at Pine Bluff, Arkansas on July 15, 1985. The West Colton–Los Angeles freights often present some rather unusual consists, and here (below) is a case in point, with a pair of SW1500's (2616 and 2461) leading a pair of non-rebuilt GP35's.

Mark A. Denis

52

SWITCHERS CONTINUED

EMD's MP15 is distinguished from the SW1500 by the hump on the roof just ahead of the cab. Southern Pacific's MP15's generally work the southeast portion of the system, as the 2694 is at Beaumont, Texas, in September 1983. *Joe Shine*

SOUTHERN PACIFIC
MP15AC

SP 2702-2731*
(SPSF 912-940)
SP 2732-2735
(SPSF 965-968)
SP 2736-2759
(SPSF 941-964)

EMD's "Dash Two" line of road locomotives incorporated solid state modular electrical systems for nearly three years before that option was offered in a switcher. Prior to 1975 all switchers used the traditional DC (direct current) generator and electrical system. The new technology was finally introduced into EMD's switchers with the unveiling of the new 1500hp MP15AC model. The center of the MP15AC's solid state electrical system is their AC/DC alternator.

The MP15AC is eighteen inches longer than its predecessor MP15, and is visually much different. The MP15AC has no front radiator grill, instead it has air intake grills on each side of the lower front carbody, much like SP's tunnel motors.

There are two types of MP15AC's on the roster, SP 2702-2731 and 2736-2759, which are regular switchers with MU connections for freight use. These switchers have been assigned to the Cotton Belt and on the SP in Texas for most of their careers.

The other four, SP 2732-2735, are equipped with the regular MU connections as well as control connections for yard slugs and creep control for hump yard duty. They were originally assigned to Roseville in November 1975 where they replaced the EMD cow and calf sets working there. The slugs had not been delivered yet so they were initially mated back-to-back with SW1200's. This combination proved a bit slippery, so the 2734 was tried with GP9 #3768 for a time. However, the combination of MP15AC's mated with SW1200's and SW1500's was the rule until July of 1979 when their slugs (SP 1010-1013) were finally delivered. The MP15AC/slug combinations have worked Roseville, Eugene and Tucson. These four are numbered separate from the other fifty-four MP15AC's in the SPSF merger. Only one MP15AC has been retired from the roster, SP 2723.

The strangest looking switchers on the roster are EMD's 1500hp MP15AC's, #2702-2759. Except for their front end, which has no radiator, they resemble the MP15. In its place are intake grills on either side which resemble those on the tunnel motors. Except for the four slug mothers, they are usually found working in Texas.
Mark A. Denis

53

CF7

Most of Santa Fe's CF7's have been sold or traded, and those that remain are stored, but a couple of years ago Los Angeles' Hobart engine facility featured a large number of CF7's. Here on a Sunday afternoon they wait for a Monday morning call to duty. These Coast Lines engines have since been replaced by 2244 class GP9's.
Mike Martin/SFSP Corp.

SANTA FE   AT&SF 2474-2648* (SPSF 1000-1060)

Perhaps the most unique type of locomotive which would have entered the merger is the highbred switcher CF7 remanufactured from EMD F3A's, F7A's and F9A's at Santa Fe's Cleburne, Texas shops between 1970 and 1978. As rebuilt, they were renumbered in reverse (below the unrebuilt GP7's) from 2649 through 2417. Altogether there were 233 CF7's constructed which was the backbone of Santa Fe's switcher fleet for many years. However, they were also used on the Eastern and Western Lines on secondary mainline freights and in local service.

During the early 1980's, and especially between 1984 and 1986, many CF7's have been retired and sold or traded. Thirty-two were traded-in to GE in December 1984, for B23-7's 6405-6418, and B39-8 7401. Perhaps the most notorious trade occurred between the Santa Fe and Amtrak in September 1984, when twenty-five CF7's, along with eighteen SSB-1200's, went to Amtrak in trade for eighteen SDP40F's.

The last of the CF7's were stored in early 1986, and as of August 1, 1986 there were only sixty-one units left on the roster, all of which were stored and were for sale.

CF7's will remain on Santa Fe property for years to come as Amtrak's units shuttle passenger cars back and forth over Santa Fe rails in Chicago and Los Angeles. Wholly owned Los Angeles Junction Railway also owns three CF7's purchased from the parent road.

After the Santa Fe was allowed to replace cabooses with an end-of-train-device many of their locals ran with pairs of CF7's (left) while their GP9's were being converted at Cleburne for five man crew operation. This local (7th Fullerton Switch) has since been powered by a single GP9.
John L. Shine

GP7

Santa Fe GP7's, #1328, 2099, 2154, 2179 and 2200 were rebuilt from units containing steam generators for passenger service and roof mounted air reservoir tanks. Although the steam boilers were removed, the tanks were left in place when rebuilt and present a rather different appearance on these five GP7's. The 1328 is equipped for service as a slug mother, but here switches Chicago's Corwith Yard alone on July 25, 1986.
John L. Shine

SANTA FE
**ATSF 2000-2027
(SPSF 1200-1227)
ATSF 2050-2243***
(SPSF 1228-1413)

Although most major roads owned substantial numbers of EMD GP7's, the huge Southern Pacific/Cotton Belt system owned but a single unit, SSW 320, later SSW 304, but it was retired and sold in November 1972. One of the major roads owning a quantity of GP7's was the Santa Fe. Originally numbered 2650 through 2893, these black and white zebra striped road switchers were to be found systemwide from Illinois to California and from Colorado to Texas. However, since the early 1960's they have been assigned to the flatlands of the Eastern and Western Lines in Illinois, Iowa, Missouri, Colorado, Oklahoma, Kansas, Texas and Louisiana.

A rebuilding program was initiated for the GP7's in 1972, continuing through 1981. During this upgrading each unit received a chopped nose, considerably altering the appearance of these switchers.

Other than the twenty 1310 class (slug mothers), there are 215 additional rebuilt GP7's, 2000-2027 and 2050-2243, which are assigned to switching and local duties on Santa Fe's lines east and north of Albuquerque and Belen, New Mexico.

A number of GP7's have been stricken from the roster and would not have enter the merger. They include the 2021, 2063, 2068, 2073, 2090, 2099, 2110, 2116 and 2133.

SANTA FE
**ATSF 1310-1329
(SPSF 1100-1119)**

Upon rebuilding, twenty GP7's were assigned as control units for yard drones, or slugs, and numbered 1310-1329. SPSF was going to number these masters in a separate series just as the Santa Fe did.

Originally built as a high nose GP7 in 1953, the 2866 entered the Cleburne Shops in November 1981, and was upgraded with new engine components, new electrical wiring, a chopped nose, an angled profile cab, a new warbonnet paint scheme, and emerged as an air conditioned slug mother #1322. Here it switches Enid, Oklahoma with slug 105 on February 18, 1984.
Mark A. Denis

GP7 CONTINUED

Only the first twenty-four GP7's were rebuilt without new "Topeka cabs", 2000-2003, 2050-2067, and slug mothers 2246-2247 (now 1310 and 1311). The 2057 and 2060 switch the yards at Argentine, Kansas in July 1984. The 2060 is fitted with an all-weather cab window on the engineers side. *Mike Start*

While the CF7's were being retired from the Coast Lines, and before the five-man-cab equipped GP9's came west, several GP7's supplemented the few remaining CF7's. Here GP7 #2074 and CF7 #2570 work a local through La Mirada, California, in February 1985.
John L. Shine

Unlike the SD39 mothers and six-axle slugs, GP7 mother 1316 and its slug 123 were painted in the merger red and yellow as a pair. The bright, eye catching duo are working at Ponca City, Oklahoma on August 26, 1986.
Thomas A. Chenoweth

Santa Fe GP7's can be found working the many locals throughout Texas. A pair of GP7's cross the MoPac diamonds at Ft. Worth's Tower 55 on a hot muggy day. The air conditioner must not be operable as the door is open to scoop up as much air as possible.
James R. Doughty

GP9

SOUTHERN PACIFIC
COTTON BELT

SP/SSW 2876-3727*
(SPSF 1700-1713)
SP/SSW 2868-3885*
(SPSF 1714-1967)

There are well over three hundred GP9's on the roster, however unlike Santa Fe's, whose complete roster of Geeps have been rebuilt, Espee has never completed the upgrading program on all of their GP9's. Southern Pacific's GP9's were delivered between 1957 and 1959, as SP 5600-5719, 5730-5844 and 5872-5891. This last group of twenty units were the only low-nose production GP9's ever produced by EMD. There were also eighty-three GP9's on the Texas & New Orleans (lettered SP), T&NO 240-249, 280-283 and 400-458, and twelve on the Cotton Belt, SSW 820-831. There were a number of differences among the many GP9's purchased by both systems. T&NO's passenger GP9's, #280-283, were transferred to the Pacific Lines in 1960, and renumbered SP 5894-5895, and 5892-5893 respectively. The steam boiler and dual controls were removed from the 5892, rendering it a freight unit for the general renumbering. The freight GP9's of the SP, T&NO and SSW were all renumbered 3400-3727 in 1965. The eleven remaining passenger Geeps were placed in the SP 3000 series.

The majority of Southern Pacific and Cotton Belt GP9's were rebuilt at Sacramento between 1970 and 1979, and placed in the 3300, 3400, 3730 and 3800 series. The 1970 and 1971 rebuilt 3300 and 3730 series have been fully amortized for tax purposes and are now candidates for retirement. The passenger GP9's were upgraded and renumbered SP 3186-3196 between 1975 and 1979.

Now to complicate the roster even more, a few rebuilt GP9's, as well as a few unrebuilt GP9's were assigned numbers in a new (for GP9's) switcher series, SP 2800's, affording these Geeps a less ambitious maintenance schedule.

During 1985 the eleven passenger GP9's were released from commute duties between San Jose and San Francisco, and are now working as local switchers, mainly in northern California.

In a program to operate some single unit locals without cabooses, the cabs of a number of GP9's have been rearranged with five seats to accomodate a full crew.

During the fall of 1978, with a shortage of switchers, Espee renumbered 17 GP9's and 15 GP9E's into the switcher series of 2868-2899. Five years later GP9E #2879 idles on the outside whisker tracks at Bakersfield, California, awaiting a call to duty. The 2879 features the non-standard Roman "SP" nose letters. *John L. Shine*

One of the first SP units to be painted in the merger scheme was GP9E #2873. Even with the new red and yellow paint there are a few non-standard features on this unit. Smaller Santa Fe style cab numbers would be adopted and white rather than clear numbers in the number boards would also be the vogue. On a cold cloudy April day in 1986, SP 2873 waits at Oil Junction to enter the mainline enroute to Bakersfield. *Mark A. Denis*

GP9 CONTINUED

There were many variations among the many orders of SP, T&NO and Cotton Belt GP9's. Here are a pair that were originally purchased for the Pacific Lines. The steam boiler equipped 3188 is one of the Geeps purchased for local passenger service, while the 3878 is from the last and only order delivered with a low-profile short hood. Both units are working through Tracy, Calif. on March 1, 1980.

Mark A. Denis

Southern Pacific GP9E #3316 reflects its Texas & New Orleans heritage with the lack of multiple signal lights. It was originally T&NO 418, becoming 3430 in 1965, and finally GP9E 3316 in June 1970. Here along with GP9E 3415, they have just worked into Mojave, California, with a local and are tied down while the crew "goes to beans", on a clear sunny December afternoon in 1985. *Joe Shine*

Cotton Belt GP9E #3813 and local caboose #1257 are tied down during the afternoon at City of Industry, California. Later the Geep will be called and work throughout the night serving the many industries along Valley Boulevard. Until recently, with the last purchase of GP40-2's, Cotton Belt did not feature their large nose initials.

Mark A. Denis

GP9 CONTINUED

There are only a very few non-rebuilt GP9's left on the SP system. Three of those, 3707-3708, and 3727, are members of the only low-nose GP9's ever built by EMD, and the last purchased by Espee. No Southern Pacific or Cotton Belt GP9 short hood was ever chopped during rebuilding, as on the Santa Fe. *John L. Shine*

Most of the Southern Pacific and Cotton Belt GP9's rebuilt between August 1973 and April 1976, were upgraded with new Farr air filters mounted in a box-like housing on the roof just ahead of the dynamic brake blister as on SP 3398 at Industry, California, in January 1986. *Mike Start*

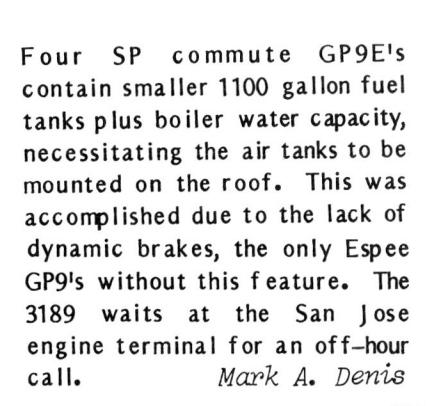

Four SP commute GP9E's contain smaller 1100 gallon fuel tanks plus boiler water capacity, necessitating the air tanks to be mounted on the roof. This was accomplished due to the lack of dynamic brakes, the only Espee GP9's without this feature. The 3189 waits at the San Jose engine terminal for an off-hour call. *Mark A. Denis*

Merger painted GP9E #3370 began its career as T&NO freight Geep #434. The tip off of its ancestry is the lack of oscillating headlights. The unit was working locals out of Bakersfield on July 6, 1986. *Don Steen*

59

GP9 CONTINUED

A pair of Santa Fe GP9's, 2251 and red/yellow 2250, work a local at Kansas City, Kansas, on July 23, 1986. The 2250 is the only merger painted GP9 working on the eastern portion of the vast Santa Fe system.
Both John L. Shine

SANTA FE
ATSF 2244-2299*
(SPSF 1968-2020)

Santa Fe's fifty-two, zebra striped GP9's, 700-751, were delivered between May 1956 and April 1957. They were renumbered in 1969/1970 in the 2900 series. They were remanufactured at Cleburne, Texas between January 1978 and Febrary 1980, and renumbered 2245-2257, 2259-2269, 2271-2287 and 2289-2299. There are also four very unique units which were upgraded as GP9's from GP7 cabless booster units, 2789A-2792A. Chopped nose cabs were added during the rebuilding program, and they were renumbered 2244, 2258, 2270 and 2288, along with the standard, chopped nosed rebuilt GP9's.

Since the early 1960's the GP9's had been assigned on the Eastern and Western Lines, however during 1985, many have been converted with five-man cabs and replaced the CF7's on the Coast Lines, mainly west of Barstow. During the spring and summer of 1986 a number have also been sent to work in California's San Joaquin Valley.

Only three, 2248-2249 and 2290, have been retired. Santa Fe's GP9's were to be renumbered beginning at SPSF 1970, due to the retirement of several SP GP9's, between March 1985 when the renumbering scheme was formed, and July 24, 1986 when the ICC disapproval was announced.

Until this past year it was very unusual for smaller units to work in consists along with "big" power on the Coast Lines. Here, at La Mirada, California, on May 17, 1986, GP9's 2268 and 2277 work as the second and third units in a five unit lashup. This has not become a widespread trend, but has been seen several times during 1986.

GP9 CONTINUED

The Coast Lines only merger painted GP9 #2291, was painted at San Bernardino in November 1985, and has been working the Los Angeles and Fullerton areas ever since. Here the "7th Fullerton Switch" waits to enter the mainline after Amtrak's "San Diegan" and "Desert Wind" have cleared.
Both Joe Shine

Although never adopted, many thought that smaller initials on the Geeps would be more appealing. With four initials this size it would have appeared to be rather crowded in. The 2291 is working industrial spurs at Buena Park, California, just west of Fullerton in November 1985.

Santa Fe acquired four GP7 cabless booster units during March and April 1953, 2789A-2792A. Upon entering the rebuilding program at Cleburne, all four were fitted with angled, air conditioned "Topeka cabs", and were upgraded to GP9 standards. They entered service as #2244, 2258, 2270 and 2288, between 1978 and 1980. Mike Start caught the 2288 working in local service between Rivera and Fullerton, California, in January 1986.

61

GP20

John L. Shine

During motive power shortages local units sometimes show up in strange places. Houston assigned non-rebuilt GP20 #4060 heads east after working as far west as Colton in June 1985.
John L. Shine

Mark A. Denis

Southern Pacific and Cotton Belt GP20's were upgraded in two manners. One group, such as the 4148 was rebuilt with its turbocharger removed, as evidenced by the dual exhausts to the front and rear of the dynamic brake fan. The 4138 was rebuilt with its turbocharger intact, and retains the unique GP20 single exhaust stack. These two Cotton Belt units also display different lettering placements. *Mike Martin*

Mike Martin

Unlike the Southern Pacific and Cotton Belt, Santa Fe rebuilt every one of their GP20's. Here three different four-axle EMD units, GP20 #3057, GP38 #2230 and GP39-2 #3138, line up outside the Amarillo, Texas, roundhouse on August 3, 1986. The 3138 (red number boards) has just been renumbered from 3638 in anticipation of the merger. *John L. Shine*

John L. Shine

62

GP20 CONTINUED

SOUTHERN PACIFIC
COTTON BELT

SP 4060-4087*
(SPSF 2975-2999)
SP 4102-4125*
(SPSF 2800-2821)
SSW 4134-4153*
(SPSF 2822-2838)

The SP system's first EMD turbocharged units were Cotton Belt's GP20's, SSW 800-809, delivered in December 1960 and January 1961. Early in 1962, the Cotton Belt took delivery of ten more, SSW 810-819, while the Espee purchased thirty-eight, including four EMD demonstrators, SP 7200-7233 and 7234-7237. During 1965 all of the GP20's were renumbered SSW 4030-4049, and SP 4050-4087.

A rebuilding program was begun in 1974 to upgrade the GP20's. Originally all were to be rebuilt with their turbochargers intact, however the first unit, SP 4100, was outshopped minus this option as a test. Meanwhile six more, SP 4101 and SSW 4134-4138, were outshopped with turbochargers intact. The test on SP 4100 proved successful so the remaining rebuilt GP20E's, SP 4102-4125 and SSW 4139-4153 were normally aspirated (minus turbochargers). The rebuilding program was terminated before all of the SP units were upgraded, so the number series 4026-4033 has always been vacant. Some have since been retired, but there were still five unrebuilt GP20's in service during 1986; SP 4060, 4063, 4079, 4085 and 4087. Upgraded GP20E's 4101, 4110, 4123, 4136, 4138 and 4145 have also been retired during the last few years. All of the GP20's and GP20E's are assigned in Texas. The unrebuilt GP20's were to become SPSF 2795-2799, while the forty remaining GP20E's were to become SPSF 2800-2839.

SANTA FE   ATSF 3000-3074*
(SPSF 2840-2910)

Santa Fe's GP20's were purchased in two groups, the first, 1100-1124, were built between May and July 1960, while the 1125-1174 were delivered between August and December 1961, for a total of seventy-five units. During the 1969/1970 renumbering program they were numbered in the 3100 series.

The GP20's have spent their entire careers on the Eastern and Western Lines, however each unit worked out to the Coast Lines at least once between January 1977 and August 1981, when each was remanufactured at the San Bernardino Shops, emerging in the 3000 series. After making several "break in" runs between Barstow and Los Angeles or San Diego, keeping them near San Bernardino, each was returned east.

Four rebuilt GP20's have been retired; 3011 in 1981, 3042 in 1984, and 3027 and 3037 in 1985.

Santa Fe GP20 #3028 is all dressed up for a wedding that is not to take place, at least not right now. The brightly painted unit is idling away the hours during a slow period on the July 4th holiday in 1986, at the east end of Bakersfield Yard.
Don Steen

This photo makes for an interesting threesome, if only coupled at the Barstow diesel facility. Here a pair of GP20's, 3033 and 3023, flank a unique SD45B unit, #5501. *Mike Martin*

GP30

COTTON BELT	SSW 5002-5009*
SOUTHERN PACIFIC	(SPSF 3000-3005)
	SP 5010-5017*
	(SPSF 3006-3012)

While EMD constructed a total of 948, 2250hp GP30's between March 1962 and November 1963, the SP system owned but a handful. The first ten came to the Cotton Belt in February 1963 as SSW 750-759, while the Espee traded in F3's for eight GP30's in March and entered service as SP 7400-7407. In 1965 all GP30's were placed in the 5000 series as SSW 5000-5009, and SP 5010-5017.

They were due for upgrading in 1975, but because of the small number of units, and because it was during a recessionary period, it was decided not to rebuild them. Many have been in and out of storage during the last few years, some have been retired, and some have been stored unserviceable and will never run again, but several were put back into service during motive power shortages during the past couple of years. SP's remaining active GP30's have all been reassigned from Pine Bluff to Houston and may be found working locals mainly in Texas and Louisiana. The thirteen GP30's which were active and/or stored serviceable during 1986, were SSW 5002-5005, 5007, 5009 and SP 5010-5013 and 5015-5017.

SANTA FE	ATSF 2700-2785
	(SPSF 3300-3379)

As scarce as GP30's are on the Espee system, Santa Fe went in the opposite direction by ordering a total of eighty-five units, paid for in part by FT trade-ins, during 1962 and 1963. Originally numbered 1200-1284, in 1969 they were placed in the 3200 series.

The Cleburne, Texas shops began rebuilding the GP30's in June 1980, releasing them without being renumbered, as there were still a number of non-rebuilt GP7's in the 2700 series. By January 1982, the GP7's had all been renumbered, and the rebuilt GP30's now received their 2700 series numbers. All GP30's rebuilt after January 1, 1982 received 2700 series numbers upon being upgraded. Santa Fe's rebuilt GP30's are now rated at 2500hp making them compatable with their GP35's.

The 1206 and 1266 were retired prior to renumbering, the 3230, 3249, 3258 and 3261 were retired prior to being rebuilt, and no rebuilt GP30 has been retired as of the end of 1986.

A major shift had transpired with the assignment of the GP30's during 1985 and 1986. With the retirement of the CF7's many GP9 switchers have been reassigned to the Coast Lines with many of the GP30's being reassigned from Coast Line road power to the Western Lines as switchers.

Santa Fe acquired an additional GP30 with the Toledo Peoria & Western in January 1984, when red and white TP&W 700 became AT&SF 3285. The unit was rebuilt at Cleburne in July 1984, and became GP30u, Santa Fe 2785.

During a shortage of motive power in November 1985, Cotton Belt #5005 showed up in West Colton, California. While the GP30's once roamed the main-lines, they now have worked in local service in the southeast for many years. *Mike Start*

One of the Houston assigned GP30's working out of Dalhart, Texas on the old Rock Island mainline rests between switching assignments on the BN interchange at this location, on July 16, 1985. *John L. Shine*

GP30 CONTINUED

A Cajon Pass helper set consisting of red GP30 #2720 and re-renumbered GP35 #2805 idle in the afternoon sun at San Bernardino on August 2, 1986. From mid-June until late July the 2805 carried post-merger number 3564. *Joe Shine*

James R. Doughty

GP30's usually operate with other Geeps, but occasionally one can be found working with 6-axle units. Such is the case with GP30 #2771 along with a SD45 and SD45-2 at Devore on November 2, 1985. *Joe Shine*

GP30 #2718 (top right) is working in local service between Albuquerque and Belen, New Mexico, in August 1985. While the 2718 is working alone, two GP30's and a pair of GP35's (below) are assigned to work with the steel gang on a ribbon rail train in the desert east of Barstow. *Mike Martin/SFSP Corp.*

GP35

SOUTHERN PACIFIC	SP 4160, SSW 4200-4203
COTTON BELT	(SPSF 2950-2954)
	SSW 6501-6519*
	(SPSF 3400-3412)
	SP 6521-6679*
	(SPSF 3413-3484)
	SSW 6680-6681
	(SPSF 3485-3486)
	SP 6300-6361*
	(SPSF 3500-3560)

EMD's GP35's would have been well represented in the merged railroad. Originally, the Southern Pacific rostered 160 of these 2500hp locomotives, Cotton Belt owned 22, while the Santa Fe ordered 161.

The Southern Pacific and Cotton Belt GP35's came during 1964 and 1965, just prior to the general renumbering program. Espee's were originally numbered above their GP30's, as SP 7408-7484, and SP 7700-7782, likewise Cotton Belt's were also numbered above their GP30's as SSW 760-781. During 1965 the GP35's were renumbered SSW 6500-6519, SP 6520-6679 and SSW 6680-6681. There are still approximately eighty unrebuilt GP35's on the roster which were to be numbered in the SPSF 3400 series.

Southern Pacific's prototype GP35 rebuild, the 6300, was outshopped in October 1977, with its original EMD 567 series prime mover, with components from EMD's newer 645 series engines. Five GP35's, one Espee and four Cotton Belt, were then rebuilt with new nonturbocharged 645E engines, rated at 2000hp. Essentially then, SP 4160 and SSW 4200-4203 are GP38's in a GP35 carbody. The 4160 was to have become SP 6301, so that number was left blank. However, sixty more GP35's, 6302-6361, were upgraded by contract shops. Morrison-Knudsen's Boise shops rebuilt thirty-four units between October 1978 and November 1979, while Canadian National's Montreal shops upgraded another twenty-six units between January and December 1979.

A number of both rebuilt and unrebuilt GP35's have been converted with five-man crew cabs for local service without cabooses. After being converted they entered the paint shop at Sacramento for the new SPSF scheme. The initial units so equipped and painted were: unrebuilt GP35's; 6533, 6566, 6577, 6606, 6619, 6640 and 6644; and rebuilt GP35's 6304, 6322, 6354, 6356 and 6361.

Five units, Southern Pacific 4160 and Cotton Belt 4200–4203, are the only GP35's rebuilt with new EMD 645E prime movers, most of the remaining rebuilt GP35's were upgraded by Morrison-Knudsen at Boise, Idaho (35 units), or Canadian National at their Montreal Works (25 units). The five units rebuilt with 2000hp 645E engines do not have turbochargers, thus the dual exhaust stacks. Cotton Belt 4200 is on a transfer cut to the Family Lines in New Orleans in September 1983. Espee #4160 is arriving at West Colton on a freight from Bakersfield in August 1985. *Both Joe Shine*

GP35 CONTINUED

Cotton Belt 6681 (the highest numbered GP35) is in charge of the Anaheim Hauler with an interesting consist. 6681-1517-1502-7662-1506-1516 (GP35/2 SD7's/GP40-2/2 SD7's) have just picked up Valla containers at Industry, and will take the hauler only as far east as West Colton. *John L. Shine*

SP 6644 is one of the GP35's rearranged to accomodate a five-man crew, and is on its way back to the southeast for local service when photographed at Bakersfield on April 26, 1986. *Mark A. Denis*

The 6300 was SP's prototype GRIP rebuild which kept its original prime mover. The remaining 6300 class (6302-6361) were rebuilt by Morrison-Knudson or Canadian National. *Mark A. Denis*

Morrison Knudson rebuild #6340 is working with a SD45 and GP9 on a ribbon rail train at Beaumont, California. Notice the large numbers in the number boards on all M-K GP35 rebuilds. *Joe Shine*

67

GP35 CONTINUED

SANTA FE
ATSF 2801-2964*
(SPSF 3561-3718)

Santa Fe's first order of GP35's, 1300-1349, came from EMD-FT trade-ins, between January and June 1964. A second group, consisting of 101 units, were delivered during 1965, and were numbered 1350-1460. The 1300 and 1320 were retired prior to the 1969 general renumbering, so the remaining GP35's were renumbered 3301-3319, and 3321-3460. During the fourth quarter of 1978 the remanufacturing program was begun for the GP35's. The first twenty rebuilds retained their original numbers until January 1982, when slots were made available by the renumbering of remanufactured GP7's and GP9's. The 3317, 3395 and 3450 were retired prior to being rebuilt, so the rebuilt GP35's were renumbered 2801-2816, 2818-2819, 2821-2894, 2896-2949 and 2951-2960. The 2803 and 2926 have been retired since being rebuilt.

When the TP&W was acquired on January 1, 1984, three GP35's, TP&W 900-902, and a single GP40, TP&W 1000, came to the Santa Fe. Upon their arrival these red and white units were renumbered AT&SF 3462-3464, and 3461 respectively. They all entered the San Bernardino Shops in late 1984, and emerged as standard Santa Fe rebuilt GP35's, numbered 2961-2964. The GP40 (2964) was derated to 2500hp and is actually a rebuilt GP35, distinguished only by the three large fans to the rear of the long hood, instead of the two large and one small, as on standard GP35's. The GP35 rebuild program was concluded in January 1985.

During the last week in June 1986, Santa Fe began renumbering their #2801-2842 GP35's into the SPSF 3561-3599 slot, which at that time was unoccupied. Most had been renumbered into the 3561 series when the ICC's decision was rendered. Shortly thereafter Santa Fe began renumbering them back to their 2800 series numbers.

This photo suggests how confusing the painting and numbering had become by June and July 1986. This Tehachapi helper set contains GP35 #3582, old paint, new number; GP35 #3592, new paint, new number; GP35 #2837, new paint, old number; followed by a GP30 #2751, old paint, old number.
Don Steen

Classification lights, the pair of small lights on the nose which contained three color designators; clear for running extra, green for a second section following, or red when operating as the rear unit, such as pushers, were deemed unnecessary by the governmental agency which regulated such matters. The railroads (both SP and ATSF) have been removing them at a rapid pace, such was the case with red and yellow GP35 #2946 at San Bernardino on May 10, 1986. *John Shine*

68

GP35 CONTINUED

Quite a few Santa Fe GP35's received merger paint, but 2848 photographed at Oklahoma City on July 27, 1986, is one that also was outfitted with air intake shields and smoke deflectors.
Thomas A. Chenoweth

A quartet of GP35's work the First District Local east from San Bernardino on April 26, 1986 at Keenbrook in Cajon Pass. The track curving to the right in the foreground is a new interchange track which, if the merger goes through, will handle Barstow (ATSF)-West Colton (SP) traffic. *John L. Shine*

When Santa Fe took complete control of the Toledo, Peoria & Western in January 1984, this lone GP40 became their property. TP&W 1000 became AT&SF 3461 in January 1984, and upon remanufacture at San Bernardino it had been derated to 2500hp as a standard GP35 and renumbered AT&SF 2964. Note the three large fans to the rear on the long hood.
Mark A. Denis

Santa Fe's GP35's have always been common on the Coast Lines both in switching and local service, while rather rare on the eastern portion of the system. Here #2893 switches a cut of grain hoppers at Ono in the shadow of the San Bernardino Mountains in March 1986.
John L. Shine

GP38

Some of the most interesting motive power lashups may be found moving through a yard area. Such is the case on May 10, 1986, at Barstow with GP38 #2307 leading GP9 #2260 and SD39 #1558. The pair of Geeps are enroute to new locations but the SD39 calls this desert yard home. *John L. Shine*

Santa Fe GP38's are usually more at home on the Eastern and Western Lines but #2316 is working on the Coast Lines at Bakersfield on September 2, 1985, moving a lumber load onto an eastbound cut. *Joe Shine*

SANTA FE   ATSF 2300-2360*
                                         (SPSF 2300-2358)

Santa Fe's sixty-one, 2000hp GP38's were purchased in 1970 for secondary freights mainly on the Eastern and Western Lines. After nearly fifteen years of service these 3500 class units were ready for upgrading at Santa Fe's Cleburne, Texas shops. The remanufacturing program began in September 1984, and was concluded in August 1985, with the units emerging as the 2300 class with many GP38-2 components. There are only fifty-nine rebuilt GP38's rostered, as the 3523 and 3552 were retired prior to being rebuilt.

SANTA FE   ATSF 2370-2380
                                         (SPSF 2400-2410)

The Toledo Peoria & Western became part of the Santa Fe in January 1984, and with it came eleven EMD GP38-2's, TP&W 2001-2011, built during 1977 and 1978. They retained their red and white paint scheme during the first couple months on the Santa Fe, but were renumbered AT&SF 3561-3571. The shops at Kansas City began painting the units into Santa Fe's familiar blue with yellow warbonnet in April of 1984. During the spring of 1985 the eleven units were renumbered into the 2370 class.

Unlike Santa Fe's rebuilt GP38's, or Southern Pacific's GP38-2's, these ex-TP&W GP38-2's do not have dynamic brakes, and until recently they did not have cab air conditioners.

Santa Fe red and yellow GP38-2 #2370 (ex-TP&W) is assigned to Albuquerque, New Mexico, on May 26, 1986. These eleven GP38-2's (2370-2380) are easily identifiable by the lack of dynamic brakes, the only second generation units on the Santa Fe without this feature. Within the last year they have been equipped with cab air conditioners. *Mike Start*

GP38-2

In 1980 SP purchased their first medium-horsepower 4-axle units; 15 GE B23-7's, and 45 EMD GP38-2's. Both types were originally assigned in Texas and Arkansas, but recently some of the GP38-2's have been reassigned in California. At Dalhart, Tex. the 4825 (right) is the local unit assigned, while SD40T-2 #8248 has been set out of an eastbound manifest and is waiting to be picked up by a westbound, on July 22, 1986. Below, almost one year earlier at the same location El Paso based GP38-2 #4842 awaits a call to duty. *John L. Shine*

SOUTHERN PACIFIC SP 4800-4811 (SPSF 2411-2455)

Espee entered the market for GP38-2's in 1980, ordering forty-five. Upon delivery most were stored for a short while due to unfavorable business conditions. On entering service they were assigned to Houston, then later El Paso, however during 1985 and 1986, many have been reassigned to Roseville and Los Angeles for local service throughout many portions of California.

John L. Shine

Four GP38-2's, 4839-4841 and 4843, specially equipped for snow removal service have swapped trucks with GP40M's (SSW 7960 series) giving the 4800's four brake cylinders per truck instead of two, which is normal for GP38-2's. The 4839 is equipped with a custom built shield to keep snow from piling up on the nose, a horn heater, icicle breakers on the roof, rotary windshield wipers and Farr air intake shrouds. *Joe Shine*

GP39-2

SANTA FE ATSF 3600-3705*
(SPSF 3100-3202)

A very popular medium powered locomotive on the Santa Fe, if not on many other roads, is EMD's 2300hp GP39-2. There were six orders placed between August 1974 and April 1980, for a total of 106 units, 3600-3705, with 103 remaining on the roster. The 3648, 3672 and 3692 were retired and scrapped in 1983 and 1984.

In an ongoing program to upgrade all older locomotives, Santa Fe began remanufacturing the GP39-2's at their Cleburne Shops during the second half of 1986. This rebuilding program will lap over into 1987. The original group, 3600-3616, was obtained during the summer of 1974 on a lease deal and will not be upgraded at this time. They were renumbered 3100-3116 during June and July 1986 in anticipation of a merger approval, and had the distinction of being the first unrebuilt locomotives to receive new SPSF numbers.

At our roster date nine units had been retired for the rebuilding program; 3622, 3625, 3631, 3653, 3666, 3668, 3674-3675 and 3689. The first GP39-2 to be rebuilt was the 3631 which was outshopped at Cleburne during August 1986, as blue and yellow Santa Fe #3400.

All of the GP39-2's which had already received their post-merger 3100 series numbers, and had not yet been retired for rebuilding, where renumbered back to their original 3600 series Santa Fe numbers.

The GP39-2's have spent their years serving on the Eastern and Western Lines mainly as road switchers, and working on local and secondary freights.

The old and new meet northeast of Albuquerque, New Mexico as GP39-2 #3698 assists Amtrak's Southwest Chief past a semaphore signal, which many years earlier gave Santa Fe's first diesels a clear block for the Super Chief. *James R. Doughty*

John L. Shine

Santa Fe's GP39-2's were the first non-rebuilt diesels to be renumbered for the merger. Above, blue #3138, with red number boards, sits on the garden tracks at Amarillo, Texas on August 3, 1986, while the 3632 (original number) left, has a new coat of red and yellow at Topeka, Kansas on April 22, 1986. *Thomas A. Chenoweth*

72

GP40M GP40-2M

SOUTHERN PACIFIC/COTTON BELT SP 7940-7959*
(SPSF 4000-4018)
SSW 7960-7967
(SPSF 4019-4026)

After extensive testing with a borrowed Seaboard Coast Line GE U23B-Mate-U23B set in 1977, Espee decided to operate Tractive Effort Booster Units (TEBU) on certain high tonnage branch lines, especially in Arizona, Texas and Oregon. The first group of "mother" units, brand new GP40-2's, were delivered in May 1980, as SP 7940-7959. The prototype TEBU, SP 1600, was constructed by Morrison-Knudsen from a cut down Union Pacific GE U25B. It was also delivered to the Espee in May 1980, and mated with the 7940 and 7941. They worked extensively on branch lines in Arizona while the Sacramento Locomotive Works constructed thirteen more TEBU's to be mated with GP40-2's, SP 7942-7959, and eight 1966 era Cotton Belt GP40's which were rebuilt and emerged from S.L.W. as SSW 7960-7967. These eight GP40's were originally SSW 7600-7607, built in January 1966. As rebuilt, between January and June 1982, they are now mechanically and electrically identical to the original SP GP40-2 mother units.

One of SP's units, #7957, was retired in 1982 due to wreck damage.

The first group of GP40-2M's, slug mothers, were purchased for drag freight service in the mining areas of Arizona. A pair of GP40-2's plus one 1600 series slug were intended to take the place of a four unit set of GP35's, with the resultant fuel efficiency. El Paso assigned GP40-2M SP 7951 and TEBU 1605 are working out of Tucson on September 7, 1981.

Both Mark A. Denis

Cotton Belt GP40 #7602 was rebuilt at the Sacramento Locomotive Works to GP40-2 specifications and emerged as slug mother SSW 7961 during the first half of 1982. Here at West Colton in May 1982, mated with TEBU SP 1610 and SSW 7960, the set is on its way to the southeast and their first assignment.

GP40P-2

SOUTHERN PACIFIC   SP 3197-3199
                        (SPSF 4100-4102)

With the pending retirement of the last of the Fairbanks-Morse Trainmasters from the San Francisco-San Jose commute pool, in 1974, Southern Pacific ordered three steam boiler equipped, 3000hp locomotives in the form of EMD's GP40P-2's. They were intended to bolster the fleet of eleven passenger GP9's, two passenger SD9's and ten SDP45's, and were numbered between the rebuilt GP9's, and the SDP45's as SP 3197-3199. The three units were delivered in November 1974, and were operated in freight service for several months prior to entering the demanding commute service. The three units strayed from the Bay Area from time to time, especially the red, white and blue Bi-centennial 3197, to power some of the business specials. They could also be found working freight on weekends and holidays.

Cal-Trans F40's replaced all of Espee's commute units during 1985, so the GP40P-2's are now working freights on a permanent basis.

During October 1986, the three GP40P-2's were renumbered SP 7600-7602.

After working freight out of Roseville for several months, GP40P-2 SP 3198, stops off at West Colton in November 1985, enroute to San Antonio, Texas to work the Eagle Pass branch, which is a connection with the NdeM.   *Mike Start*

Best known for their assignment as commute units in the San Francisco-San Jose pool, GP40P-2's often strayed far from home on business specials as seen here in Beaumont Pass on February 18, 1979, powered by 3199 and 3198. The third member of the class, SP 3197, was even more notorious for leaving the Bay Area on specials, as it was painted red, white and blue for the bicentennial during the mid and late 1970's.   *Mark A. Denis*

GP40-2

SOUTHERN PACIFIC
COTTON BELT

SP/SSW 7608-7677*
(SPSF 4103-4169)
SP/SSW 7240-7273
(SPSF 4170-4203)

The first EMD four-axle freight power ordered by the Southern Pacific in twelve years came during March and April of 1978, as GP40-2's SP 7608-7627. Visibly they looked very much like the original Cotton Belt GP40's of 1966, but they contained all of the dash 2 amenities, most importantly is the state of the art wheel-slip controls. Thirty more were delivered between January and March of 1979 for the Cotton Belt, SSW 7628-7657, followed by another twenty for the Southern Pacific in March and April 1980, SP 7658-7677. During 1984 a power hungry Espee went back for still more GP40-2's, eight for the parent road, plus twenty-six for the Cotton Belt. SSW 7248-7273 were delivered first, during the fourth quarter of 1984, followed closely by SP 7240-7247, during November. It was believed that this would be the last EMD units purchased by the Southern Pacific/Cotton Belt, but with the ICC disapproval of July 24, 1986 only time will tell.

Only one GP40-2 received the new red and yellow bonnet scheme, SP 7672. On August 20, 1986, the GP40-2 leads a pair of GE B30-7's #7842 and 7833, on a westbound general freight through Industry, California.

All John L. Shine

A pair of GP40-2's, Cotton Belt 7634 and Southern Pacific 7660, lead the ESKCQ (East St. Louis-Kansas City Sprint) on MoPac track at Gratiot St. Tower in St. Louis on July 23, 1986. This train will travel on trackage rights obtained through the UP-MP-WP merger in December 1984.

Cotton Belt 7266 leads a pair of SD45's and a GP40-2 through Industry, Ca. in December 1985, with the GMWCY (Gemco-West Colton General Freight). This newest batch of Cotton Belt GP40-2's have the large initials on the nose as well as small initials on the anticlimber, neither of which grace the front of SSW 7634 above.

GP40X

SOUTHERN PACIFIC   SP 7200-01,30-31
(SPSF 4400-4403)

There were only twenty-three "Super Series" 3000hp EMD GP40X's built between December 1978 and December 1979. If the merger would have been consummated over one-half of all the GP40X's ever constructed would have been on the SPSF. Actually, the first units went to the Union Pacific in December of 1977, followed by four for the Southern Pacific in February 1978, while ten went to the Santa Fe during April and May 1978, the most owned by any road.

The four which were purchased by the Southern Pacific were uniquely SP, with "elephant ears" to shield the air intake grills, EMD's new HT-B trucks, and oscillating light packages, both front and rear. The tunnel shields were for testing in the snowsheds and tunnels of the Sierras, and did not render enough cooling outside the tunnels, so these shields were removed. The GP40X's were also equipped as radio controlled units; 7200-7201 RCE masters and 7230-7231 RCE remotes.

If any Espee GP40X's had been painted in the merger red and yellow scheme they would have been very distinguishable from Santa Fe's, as the SP units were equipped with EMD HT-B trucks, larger snowpilots and the usual multi-light package fore and aft.

Mark A. Denis

All four SP GP40X's usually operate together out of West Colton on the many haulers into the Los Angeles basin. The 7201 leads 7200, 7231 and 7230 through Los Nietos, California, enroute to West Colton. A portion of the route will be over trackage rights on Union Pacific's mainline from Bartolo to Puente Junction, almost seven miles.

John L. Shine

GP40X CONTINUED

SANTA FE
ATSF 3800-3809
(SPSF 4404-4413)

The GP40X's were the test beds for EMD's new "Super Series" diesels. After extensive testing it was hoped that the railroads would clamor for their successor the GP50, however the Santa Fe and Southern were the only two roads which owned the GP40X's to also purchase GP50's. However several roads which tested the GP40X's (not owners), did buy substantial numbers of GP50's, including the Burlington Northern and Frisco.

Santa Fe's ten GP40X's, 3800-3809, were ordered with EMD's standard Blomberg-M trucks. The 3800 is equipped as an RCE master, while the 3801 is a receiver unit, the only Santa Fe GP40X's so equipped.

Santa Fe's hottest train the 991 (Richmond-Chicago) almost always rates four units, as on August 21, 1985 at Mountainair, New Mexico, with two GP40X's followed by a pair of GP50's. After a visit to one of Santa Fe's paint booths GP40X #3801 now sports a lower cigar-band nose herald. *Don Steen*

Only two GP40X's had been painted in the merger scheme, one the 3805 (right) and the other #3803, which had already been repainted back into Santa Fe's standard blue and yellow by September 1986, when this photo was taken. *John L. Shine*

On September 9, 1979, RCE master GP40X #3800 is in charge of seven such units on the York Canyon-Fontana unit coal train destined for Kaiser's steel mill just west of San Bernardino. The only GP40X so equipped is in control of RCE receiver #3801 mid-train with three additional GP40X's.

Mike Martin/SFSP Corp.

77

GP50

SANTA FE   **ATSF 3810-3854**
                        (SPSF 4500-4544)

The first group of 3500hp EMD GP50's came to the Santa Fe between January and April 1981, numbered above their ten GP40X's, as 3810-3839. Fourteen units came equipped as Locotrol remote radio sets; 3810-3822 (even) are masters, or lead units; 3811-3823 (odd) are receivers. The 3824-3839 from the first order, and fifteen more, 3840-3854, which came in May 1985, did not contain RCE equipment. There are a few differences between the two groups. The 1985 units came with EMD's new standard freeflow blower bulge on the left side of the locomotive, and this group also has a plate on the top of the nose for easier access to the facilities located in the nose.

Santa Fe GP50 #3819, from the class of 1981, shows off a rather plain nose after the classification lights have been plated over. Notice the difference between the blower ducts on this unit, and the newer (1985) GP50 #3851, below.
Joe Shine

A pair of brand new, spotless GP50's and Santa Fe Ten-Pack fuel foiler trailer flats pose for an official photograph at LA's Hobart Yard in May 1985. The railroad is very proud of their new equipment and rarely miss an opportunity to promote the same to shippers.
Mike Martin/SFSP Corp.

One year old GP50 #3851 is in charge of one of Santa Fe's fast Bay Area-Kansas City trains through the Tehachapi Mountains in August 1986. The almost-look-alike GP40X which follows is distinguished by the flared rear radiator grills.
Don Steen

GP50 CONTINUED

The eastbound 991 train (Richmond–Chicago) coasts downhill toward Mojave, California, with a long train of loaded "pigs". Todays train boasts a consist of five units with GP50 #3827 in the lead followed by a GP40X, SDF45 and a pair of SD40-2's. *Mike Martin*

Santa Fe has a power pool of high horsepower 4-axle units assigned almost exclusively to their hot, fast COFC and TOFC cross country trains. One of these trains with four 3500hp GP50's is climbing Cajon Pass in the early morning passing a Southern Pacific eastbound lumber drag bound for Colton on June 14, 1986. *John L. Shine*

SD7

Before being rebuilt during 1979, many of the SD7's contained a myriad of oscillating headlights. Today most of the forty-two units contain this five light package with a red emergency oscillating light on the top, dual amber oscillating lights, and below dual fixed sealbeam headlights as on the 1526 at Roseville. *Mark A. Denis*

SOUTHERN PACIFIC SP 1500-1542
(SPSF 1500-1542)

Southern Pacific's original six-axle road switchers (SP 5200-5278) were from Baldwin, however SP was also an early customer of six-axle EMD power in the form of 1500hp SD7's which were delivered between November 1952 and January 1953 as SP 5279-5293. All except the 5288 and 5289 were leased to the Northwestern Pacific initially. The distinguishing feature of these first black and orange tiger striped units was the single 1200 gallon fuel tank. The group that followed, SP 5309-5335 and EMD demonstrator 5308, came equipped with a Vapor model 4625 steam boiler for occasional use on local and commute passenger trains. These units carried an extra 1200 gallon water tank for the steam generator. When the steam equipment was removed during the late 1950's these tanks were converted to carry fuel. After the SD9's were delivered in the "black widow" scheme all of the SD7's were repainted in this scheme upon shopping.

During the late 1950's and early 1960's they lost their "black widow" scheme to the more demure gray with scarlet ends. In 1965, during the system renumbering program, they became SP 2700-2742. They were renumbered once again as a group in 1973, to 1400-1442, to make room for new EMD MP15 switchers.

The years and miles caught up with the SD7's, and by January 1979, Sacramento General Shops began upgrading them to SD7E's, renumbering them in the 1500 series.

Through the years they have seen assignments on local passenger trains and mainline helper duties, but are now assigned to local freight, transfer cuts and heavy yard duties. These 1500hp road switchers have never wandered far from California, and are the only group of units purchased during the 1950's that are still intact.

Most of the SD7's can be found in the Roseville and LA-Colton areas of California, working heavy switching and local drag and hauler freights. The 1508 and 1534 are tied up at the west end of Industry after working a cut from Valla with loaded trailer flats.
John L. Shine

SD9

Los Angeles assigned SD9 #4347 has been working the Industry area and is MU'ed with merger painted SP 4418 on September 20, 1986. When mixed with SP's gray and red units these bright machines are very prominent.
Mike Start

SOUTHERN PACIFIC
SP 4301-4451*
(SPSF 5000-5134)

The next step in progression after EMD dropped the SD7 from their catalog was the SD9, a very successful locomotive on the SP. The Cadillacs, as they are referred to by many of the crews, because of their smooth riding qualities, came with a revised 567C engine and D37 traction motors. The horsepower yield is 1750 compared to 1500 on the SD7's.

These machines were purchased for and assigned to road service mainly on the stiff mountain grades of Oregon and California. Some were subsequently assigned to the Northwestern Pacific where solid five and six unit sets were common.

The Pacific Lines, i.e. west of El Paso, Texas, was the only segment of the system to receive the SD7's and SD9's.

The SD9's numbered 149 and were delivered between 1954 and 1956. Unlike the SD7's, the SD9's were all delivered in the famous black widow paint scheme. They were assigned road numbers SP 5340-5444, and 5449-5493. Alco RSD-5's were numbered below, in between, and above the SD9 number blocks. All of that came to an end in 1965 when the remaining SD9's were renumbered SP 3800-3966.

Sacramento's rebuilding program was initiated on the SD9's in 1970 and continued through 1980. They are now numbered SP 4300-4441, along with a pair of steam boiler equipped units SP 4450 and 4451. This upgrading was intended to give the units an additional ten to twelve years of service, however some would have been entering the merger with almost sixteen additional years, and are still going strong.

Unlike the SD7's, the SD9's have had a few members retired through the years. The 5358 and 5482 were retired in 1963 and 1964 respectively, while the 5456 and 5458 were retired in 1966, all prior to being renumbered. The 3961 and 3953 were retired in 1966 and 1970 respectively. This left a total of 143 units to be rebuilt out of a total of 149 original SD9's. The 4321 was the first rebuilt unit to depart the roster in 1982, followed by the 4300, 4309 and 4388 all during 1984, and the 4308 in 1986. The Southern Pacific leased out the operation of their Tillamook Branch in Oregon to the Port of Tillamook Bay, and with it went three more SD9's #4368, 4381 and 4414. The 4381 had been repainted in the new SPSF yellow bonnet scheme and was the first diesel in the new paint to depart the roster.

Most of the SD9's have always called California and Oregon home, however a pair, 4359 and 4375, have been assigned to Houston for a number of years where they work in yard and local service. During the spring of 1986 the 4375 was returned to Sacramento for routine maintenance, repainted in the new red/yellow scheme, and returned to Houston.

Southern Pacific's SD7's and SD9's are the only high nose, six axle units which would have entered the merger, as the Santa Fe did not own either type. The 4363 holds the honors as being the first high-hood SD to be repainted in the red/yellow bonnet scheme.

There was a time, quite a number of years ago, when SD9's ruled these mountain passes on long, heavy tonnage. However, today about the only time one climbs this curve at Walong in the Tehachapi's is in work train service as does the 4311 on December 14, 1985.
Mark A. Denis

SD9 CONTINUED

The quiet is temporarily broken as a freight descends down Santa Margarita Hill bound for San Luis Obispo, California, on the Coast Line. With dynamics screaming three SD9's lead with two more SD9's and a pair of SD45T-2's mid-train, hold back tonnage on the 2.2% ruling grade. *Mike Martin*

Two SD9's, 4450 and 4451 above, retained their steam boilers for stand-by passenger service. Such is the case on a rainy February day in 1985, as the pair make a station stop at Santa Clara with the three car Cal-Train commute #51. *Paul Lukens*

Below 4361 and 4440 run out of Mojave for a day on the mountain with a work train on this cold January day in 1985, at Monolith, California. *Joe Shine*

SD26

SANTA FE ATSF 4600-4679*
(SPSF 5400-5434)

Santa Fe's first EMD six-motor freight units, the 2400hp SD24's, were purchased in two orders. The original group, 900-944, were delivered in May and June 1959, while the second group, 945-979, came one year later between May and July 1960.

All eighty units were still intact for the 1969/1970 general renumbering when they received 4500 series numbers.

The remanufacturing program, which began in January 1970, gave each engine new components from EMD's modern 645 engine assemblies, replaced each unit with new traction motors, extended range dynamic brakes, rebuilt generators, as well as upgraded wiring. They emerged from the shops as SD26's rated at 2650hp. They received the yellow bonnet paint scheme as did a few 4500's which were repainted between June 1972 and the date each was shopped. The rebuilding program was finally completed at San Bernardino Shops in January 1978.

The 4625 was retired during the summer of 1974, but the remaining seventy-nine SD26's ran out their years until early 1985 when forty-four units were traded in to EMD for fifteen new GP50's, 3840-3854.

During the last few years many of the SD26's have been in and out of storage and some have been in yard service at Kansas City and Barstow. In the yards they have worked alone, paired together, paired with GP35's, and mated with yard slugs.

At the end of 1985 there were thirty-five SD26's on the roster, most of which were stored serviceable, with only a couple still pulling yard duty. During February 1986 even these were set aside when replaced by freshly rebuilt 1556 class SD39's.

The remaining SD26's probably would not have physically been renumbered in the SPSF series as they are all stored and are just trade-in bait.

The days were numbered for the SD26's in road service when photographed waiting for a block signal at Fullerton, California, on August 23, 1984. Many of the series had already been stored, but this westbound freight is powered by 4650-4646-4655-4615-2851-5981-5311 (four SD26's/GP35/SDF45/SD45).
John L. Shine

SD26's had been banned from the road, but a few still worked in heavy yard service at Argentine and Barstow in November 1985. Within the month the 4627 and 4676 will be replaced by newly rebuilt SD39's in this service. When photographed the SD39's were already testing in road and local service on the Coast Lines. *Joe Shine*

83

SD35

SOUTHERN PACIFIC

SP 3106-3109
(SPSF 1576-1579)
SP 3102-3105*
(SPSF 1580-1582)
SP 2961-2970
(SPSF 1583-1592)

Espee's twenty-nine SD35's, purchased in 1964 and 1965, were the first six-axle power to be ordered since 1959, and the first from EMD since 1956. They were powered by EMD's 567-turbocharged engine rated at 2500hp. They were delivered just prior to the general renumbering as SP 4816-4844, but were soon renumbered SP 6900-6928. Initially their assignment was the L.A.-Bakersfield freight pool where they worked with EMD SD9's and Alco DL701's over the Tehachapi Mountains.

Without exception, SP's SD35's, as a group, are the most renumbered units on the roster. Between April and October 1974, four SD35's were upgraded with new electrical components, new wiring and updated turbocharged prime movers, and were renumbered SP 6950-6953 as SD35E's. Then the rebuilding program for SD35's ceased. Between 1976 and 1978, ten more 6900's were rebuilt by replacing their 2500hp 567-engines with normally-aspirated 2000hp 645-engines. This group was now functionally identical to an SD-38, and they were renumbered 4700-4709. The 4700 was numbered 6954 briefly. In December of 1979 this group was again renumbered, SP 2961-2970 for hump service at Houston's Englewood Yard. Also in late 1979, SD35E's, 6950-6953, as well as unrebuilt SD35's, 6919, 6924, 6927 and 6928 were renumbered SP 3102-3109 respectively for West Colton yard service. The 3104 has been retired.

Assigned to Los Angeles for maintenance but used almost exclusively at West Colton SD35's 3106-3109, and SD35E's 3102-3105, usually perform trim work, i.e. putting together humped cars into a finished train. *John L. Shine*

Externally the 3102 and 3106 series are alike, as both retain their turbochargers, thus both have the larger single exhaust stack, unlike the 2961-2970 series which have smaller dual stacks. The 3107 idles with another SD35 in the morning sun at West Colton on April 30, 1986. *Mark A. Denis*

The ten SD35E's in the 2961-2970 series are assigned to Englewood Yard in Houston where they usually work the hump in threes, coupled elephant style and are worked from the rear unit as seen here with the 2964 in June 1984. The 2968 was sent to Sacramento for shop work during March 1986 and emerged in red and yellow merger paint and has since been sent back to Houston. *Mark A. Denis*

SD38-2

SOUTHERN PACIFIC   SP 2971-2976 (SPSF 1550-1555)

In May of 1973 Espee took delivery of six non-turbocharged units from EMD in the form of SD38-2's, SP 2971-2976. These 2000hp locomotives are in reality, super switchers, built specifically for duty at West Colton. Pairs of SD38-2's were mated with yard slugs, #1000-1002, constructed from a pair of retired Alco C-628's and a lone C-630, and worked the big yard until the slugs were retired in 1983. Since then the SD38-2's have been working in heavy yard duty at West Colton with SD7's, SD9's, SD35's, SD35E's and in pairs. Only on rare occasions do these SD38-2's venture away from West Colton, and then only as far as Los Angeles on WC-LA drags.

It is rare to find a yard hump set out on the mainline, but such is the case with 2974-4367-2972 (SD38-2/SD9/SD38-2), enroute to the old Colton yard from the big yard at West Colton in March 1986.

The six SD38-2's are all set up as "super switchers" exclusively for West Colton and are rarely used in road service. During recessionary periods, when only two sets are needed for switching, one pair has been observed working local freights.
Both John L. Shine

Since West Colton hump slugs, SP 1000-1002, have been retired and sold to Chrome Locomotive Works, several types of six-axle diesels have taken their place operating with the SD38-2's. On August 3, 1985, two sets idle briefly at the westend of the the hump; 2976-4393-4418 (SD38-2/SD9/SD9) and 2972-4322-2973 (SD38-2/SD9/SD38-2). Other types of units usually in use with the SD38-2's are SD7E's, SD35's and SD35E's. *Joe Shine*

SD39

SOUTHERN PACIFIC
SP 5300-5318*
(SPSF 5300-5311)

The SD39 is a medium sized road unit having a 12-cylinder turbocharged 645E3 engine developing 2300hp, with extremely high tractive effort. Espee purchased their first group, 5300-5317 in 1968, and assigned them to the Bakersfield-Los Angeles freight pool. Southern Pacific went back to EMD for eight more, 5318-5325, in 1970, when their assignments found them working from Bakersfield southeast to Tucson. They remained in this assignment until about 1977, when they were reassigned out of L.A. on the many local haulers, and in helper service out of San Luis Obispo, on the Coast Line.

Several were transferred to Houston to work the Englewood hump during 1977, but were soon displaced by SD35E's in early 1978, sending the SD39's back to the L.A. area.

Most of the second series, 5319-5325, were acquired on a 15-year lease and were returned to their lessor during 1985. Several from the first group, including 5301, 5303, 5305, 5307 and 5311-5313 have been retired, and unless the remaining eleven are rebuilt, which seems remote, their future appears very bleak.

Mike Start

Purchased for mountain duty mainly in the Tehachapi's the SD39's came equipped with rear snowpilots and complete rear light packages at a time when neither was standard on the SP. They have been reassigned to southern California for many years working in local service as seen in these three photos taken during early 1986.

John L. Shine

Mike Martin

86

SANTA FE
ATSF 4000-4019 (SPSF 1556-1575)

The SD39, which is a turbocharged version of the SD38, was not a very popular model on America's railroads. As noted above the Southern Pacific purchased only 26 SD39's, but the Santa Fe owned even less with total of only 20 units.

Santa Fe's SD39's, 4000-4019, were delivered in May and June 1969, and were originally assigned to Barstow to work the Kaiser coal train between York Canyon, N.M. and Fontana, California, the longest unit coal haul in the country at that time. They were replaced by the SD26's in 1973, whereupon they were reassigned to work with GE U23C's, mainly between La Junta, Colorado and El Paso, Texas.

The units were withdrawn from service early in 1985, and stored at Barstow. During the spring and summer they were moved to San Bernardino for remanufacturing. The rebuilding program for these SD39's include receptacles for m-u plugs for yard slug controls. They were the second group of rebuilt locomotives to receive new SPSF numbers. They were renumbered in the 1556-1575 series for heavy duty yard switching. The decision to repaint all locomotives in the new SPSF red w/yellow bonnet scheme was reached during November 1985, meanwhile nine remanufactured SD39's had already received the standard Santa Fe blue w/yellow bonnet, 1556/57/58/59/60/61/63/65 and 1567.

During late 1985 and early 1986, the rebuilt SD39's "broke in" in road service mainly between LA and Barstow, keeping them close to the San Bernardino Shops. Many times there were from three to five together in the same consist. In January 1986, blue #1557 leads such a consist through the high desert near Hesperia. *Mark A. Denis*

A rather colorful back end is exhibited on the merger painted SD39's with a red brake wheel stand against a yellow rear. There are plugs both front and rear for slug control. The 1562 sits in the afternoon sun at its new home, Barstow in April 1986. *John L. Shine*

Due to the shut down of raw steel operations at Kaiser's Fontana mill all of the hot slag cars were sold to a mill in the Peoples Republic of China. Here the cars, mixed with box cars for braking, move west through San Bernardino bound for the Los Angeles Harbor where they will be loaded onto ships. SD39 #1564 leads five GP30/GP35's on the slow moving train due to hot bearings, causing many of the cars to be set out enroute. *James R. Doughty*

SD40

SOUTHERN PACIFIC

SP 7300-7385*
(SPSF 5501-5585)

Espee's SD40's came in two distinct groups. The first seventy-nine were delivered in February 1966 as SP 8400-8478. Ten more of these 3000hp units were ordered in 1968, and were delivered as SP 8479-8488.

They are assigned to mainline freight duties and are as much at home in the Bay Area as in the deserts of New Mexico and West Texas.

The GRIP program for Southern Pacific's big power (SD45/SD40's) began in late 1979 with the remanufacturing of the prototype SD45E #7400. After the 7400 was thoroughly tested, the upgrading program then continued with the SD40 fleet with SP 7300 emerging from the shops in June 1980. There were forty-four rebuilt during the second half of 1980, followed by forty-two more the following year. The 8402, 8423 and 8460 were retired prior to being rebuilt, accounting for the SD40E numbering running only through SP 7385. Just one rebuilt SD40 has been retired, that being SP 7347 which was wrecked on the BN. The 7347 was the unit SP chose to be painted for the 1984 LA Summer Olympics, but had been repainted to gray and scarlet just prior to being destroyed.

In the time honored manner the fireman on Amtrak's "Coast Starlight" hoops his train orders from SP SD40 #7323 at San Jose in June 1985. During heavy traffic periods it is not unusual for units from the home road to be leased in assisting Amtrak's own units. *Paul Lukens*

Painted in the merger red and yellow, SD40 #7357 retains its SP style cab numbers, roman digits in its number boards and complete set of nose headlights, all of which would be changed in time if the merger goes through. *Joe Shine*

At press time (October 1986), there is only one active unit on the Espee with the test "Daylight" red, orange, and black scheme, SD40 #7342. The 7342 and SD45 #7399 were the only six-axle units wearing this scheme, and the latter has already been repainted in the merger scheme. *John L. Shine*

SD40 CONTINUED

SANTA FE   ATSF 5000-5019*
                         (SPSF 5586-5603)

Following Southern Pacific's first order for EMD's SD40's, the Santa Fe took delivery of their first, and only group consisting of twenty units, 1700-1719, in March and April of 1966.

During the 1969/70 general renumbering program these SD40's were renumbered in the 5000 series.

The 5011 was retired in March 1978, but the remaining nineteen were remanufactured at San Bernardino between December 1980 and December 1981, with no change of numbers. The 5015 was retired in 1986 due to wreck damage, and if the frame can be saved it will be used for the manufacture of a slug at San Bernardino Shops.

During the winter of 1985, SD40 #5003 leads a C30-7, SD40-2, U36C and SD45, up Cajon Pass near Gish on the 881 train (LA-Chicago). The SD40's of both roads are assigned to mainline service.   *James R. Doughty*

Santa Fe's SD40's were unusual in that they were not renumbered upon being rebuilt. Many SD40's were equipped with an air intake hood and smoke deflector upon being rebuilt, as is #5016 at Ash Fork, Arizona.
Mike Martin

89

SD40-2

SANTA FE   ATSF 5028-5057*
(SPSF 6000-6028)
ATSF 5058-5108
(SPSF 6043-6093)
ATSF 5141-5192
(SPSF 6094-6145)

During the mid-1970's most western roads opted for the 16-cylinder EMD SD40-2. One of the main reasons was the greater fuel economy over the 20-cylinder 3600hp SD45-2. EMD's 3000hp SD40-2, along with GE's C30-7, has become the standard road locomotive for many of the western roads during the later 1970's and 1980's. Santa Fe had the only standard SD40-2's which would have entered the merger, with 186 units on their roster, purchased between November 1977 and December 1981.

SANTA FE   ATSF 5200-5213
(SPSF 6029-6042)

One group, 5200-5213, was numbered out of sequence when delivered in October 1978, for assignment on unit coal trains originating on the Burlington Northern with destinations on the Santa Fe. This policy has been terminated and any Santa Fe SD40-2 or GE C30-7 may now be found pooled with BN coal train power, with the 5200's working the general freight pool.

On July 3, 1986, the 5208 was involved in an accident which totally destroyed the locomotive, but as of our roster date it had not yet been officially retired.

SANTA FE   ATSF 5020-5026 (Even only)
(SPSF 5700-5706 (Even only)
ATSF 5021-5027 (Odd only)
(SPSF 5701-5707 (Odd only)
ATSF 5110-5140 (Even only)
(SPSF 5708-5738 (Even only)
ATSF 5109-5139 (Odd only)
(SPSF 5709-5739 (Odd only)

Twenty units are set up as RCE master or lead radio controlled units; 5020-5026 (even only), and 5110-5140 (even only). Twenty more, 5021-5027 (odd only), and 5109-5139 (odd only) are set up as RCE receiver units, found mostly on heavy unit coal, grain and potash trains. They are distinguished from the standard SD40-2's by their large nose or snoot which houses the radio equipment.

For modelers here is a unit with all the extras. It has Oscitrol red and twin white signal lights in the short hood, and is also equipped with the air intake hood and exhaust deflectors. The 5067 is waiting for a block signal at Victorville, California, in May 1986. *John L. Shine*

Very few RCE equipped SD40-2's were painted in the merger scheme. Master units 5022, 5026 and 5132, along with receivers 5023 and 5117 were the locomotives involved. The 5023 was photographed at Oklahoma City on July 26, 1986.
Thomas A. Chenoweth

SD40-2 CONTINUED

An excellent down on photo of a straight out-of-the-box SD40-2 #5042 is presented by Mike Martin at Cajon Summit in January 1986.

All of Santa Fe's EMD six-axle remote controlled units are equipped with a large nose, or "snoot" which houses the RC equipment. These units have four Sinclair antennas; two small ones are for remote mid-train operation, and an additional small antenna is for the end-of-train device, plus the regular large Sinclair antenna for voice communication. The 5113 is waiting in one of the pair of passing sidings at Marcel in the Tehachapis on April 19, 1986.
John L. Shine

Red and yellow SD40-2 #5182 with the 358 train (KC-LA) stops at Rivera to set out auto carriers for Ford. Only the last order of SD40-2's (5170-5192) and last group of GP50's (3840-3854) have the access door on top of the short hood.
Joe Shine

SD40-2 CONTINUED

Blue SD40-2 #5108 is in charge of a pair of red rebuilt 7200 series SD45-2's and a red C30-7 on June 27, 1986. That stack of "snap track" piled up in the background is for new interchange tracks between the Santa Fe and Southern Pacific at Colton Interlocking.
Mike Start

Santa Fe SD40-2's 5058-5070 are equipped with Oscitrol red and twin amber warning lights. The pair of white lights are positioned so that each one shines slightly to either side of the right of way flashing alternately at fifty times per minute.
Don Steen

SD40-2 #5207 from the 5200-5213 series was numbered out of sequence when delivered in 1978, for assingment on BN/ATSF unit coal trains. They are now in the general freight pool as seen here at La Mirada, California, in March 1986, on the Harbor Train (Barstow-LA Harbor).

SD40T-2

SOUTHERN PACIFIC/COTTON BELT

SP/SSW 8300-8341*
(SPSF 5740-5820 even)
SP/SSW 8350-8391
(SPSF 5741-5823 odd)
SP 8489-8573
(SPSF 5825-5909)
SP 8230-8299
(SPSF 5910-5979)

Southern Pacific's initial order of SD40-2's came with their tunnel motor variation and large nose, or snoot, which housed either master or receiver radio equipment. The first of these 3000hp units came in June 1974 as masters SP 8300-8306, and receivers SP 8350-8356. Obviously this original group was successful as twenty more masters, SP 8307-8321 and SSW 8322-8326, along with twenty receivers, SP 8357-8371 and SSW 8372-8376, were delivered between January and April 1978.

Also during January and February 1978 the first ten standard SD40T-2's came to the SP as 8489-8498. They were numbered directly above their unrebuilt SD40's. Between November 1978 and March 1979, seventy-five more standard SD40T-2's were delivered as SP 8499-8573. The next order of SD40T-2's was another group of radio equipped snoots, the last units to be so equipped on the Espee, they were delivered as SP 8327-8341 (masters), and SP 8377-8391 (remotes), between March and July of 1979. Southern Pacific was not finished ordering SD40T-2's however, as one last order for seventy more standard units were delivered between March and July of 1980, as SP 8230-8299. These were the last six-axle units ordered by the Southern Pacific or Cotton Belt. The only SD40T-2 to be retired is RCE master unit #8302 so there would not have been a SPSF 5722. Also in order to begin the non-radio equipped SD40T-2's with the SPSF 5825 series there would not have been a SPSF 5824.

Southern Pacific and Cotton Belt SD40T-2's in the 8300 and 8350 series are all Radio Control masters and receivers with the large nose or "snoot". The merger scheme is very impressive on these big machines with the large yellow nose being an extra safety factor.
John L. Shine

During 1984, the "Oil Cans", Bakersfield to Los Angeles Harbor unit Tank-Train, drifts down the grade into Mojave with five 8230-8299 series SD40T-2's on the point.
Joe Shine

In July 1985, SD40T-2 #8315 leads the LABAT (Los Angeles-Bay Area/Trailers) past the San Jose depot where the crew must hoop up their train orders.
Paul Lukens

SP 8509-8283-8541-8951 (3 SD40T-2's/SD45) lead the PTMFT (Portland-Memphis/Trailers) over the Tehachapi Mountains on April 19, 1986. The dirt "road" in the background is the old shoofly built after the July 21, 1952 earthquake.   *John L. Shine*

Freshly painted SD40T-2 #8530 is in charge of a westbound freight enroute from West Colton, in August 1986. The 8530 will work only as far as Bakersfield, where it will spend the next several days in helper service.   *Don Steen*

Four six-axle SP units work through Topeka, Kansas, on Union Pacific trackage gained in 1980 when the Cotton Belt purchased Rock Island's old "Golden State" route. The train will soon be on the ex-RI track enroute to El Paso, Texas.
Mark A. Denis

SD40T-2 CONTINUED

Single six-axle pushers are common to both the Southern Pacific and Santa Fe in the Tehachapis, and on a warm summer morning in August 1986, merger painted SD40T-2 #8530 helps an eastbound drag near Cable.
Don Steen

SP 8277-7770-7499 (SD40T-2/B36-7/SD45R) pick up and set out cars at McNeil, Arkansas, for the Louisiana & North West Railroad, a road famous for operating EMD F7's into the 1980's.
John L. Shine

SD40-2's abound, both SP tunnel motors and UP regular SD40-2's. Tehachapi Summit is the location, and power is being swapped between the headend and mid-train helpers. Five units will continue on to LA with the "Oil Cans" while six units will return to Bakersfield for helper service later in the day.
James R. Doughty

SD40T-2 CONTINUED

Mark A. Denis

Cotton Belt "snoot" #8326 (above) speeds a general freight through the desert in Arizona, in January 1986. SP SD40T-2 #8568 (left) presents a sharp portrait near Cable crossovers as it leads an eastbound freight through the many curves.
Don Steen

Only the Southern Pacific could put together such a consist. North of Fresno headed for Sacramento are; 8510-2574-9201-red 7357-9355-3399-3779-3834-3383 SD40T-2/SW1500/SD45T-2/SD40/SD45T-2/4 GP9's, on February 21, 1986. *Joe Shine*

SDF40-2

SANTA FE ATSF 5250-5267
(SPSF 6500-6517)

Amtrak's first new long-distance motive power was the steam boiler equipped SDP40F's (500-539) delivered during June 1973, with the first thirty being assigned to the Santa Fe to replace leased aging F units. EMD fashioned these units after the 20 cylinder, 3600hp FP45's of the Santa Fe and Milwaukee Road except that they were equipped with 16 cylinder engines rated at 3000hp.

It is interesting to note that while the SDP40F's were being placed in service, Santa Fe's F45's and FP45's were operated in multiple with the Amtrak units on the "Super Chief" until all thirty passenger units had been delivered. Members of this first group were also assigned to Amtrak's San Diegans, running on Santa Fe track.

One hundred ten more SDP40F's were ordered and placed in service during 1974. Many from this second group eventually operated on SP rails, between LA and Portland on the "Coast Starlight", between Oakland and Ogden on the "San Francisco Zephyr", and between LA and New Orleans on the "Sunset Limited".

Tracking problems at speed on curves on some roads (other than the AT&SF and SP) developed which resulted on the SDP40F's being banned by those roads. An order for thirty more units was cancelled, and in fact by 1977, many had been returned to Amtrak to be rebuilt into the more reliable F40PH. During the early 1980's most of the remaining 37 SDP40F's were placed in storage and offered for sale.

In a rather surprising move by Santa Fe, during mid-1984, a trade was negotiated with Amtrak which gave the passenger carrier 25 CF7's and 18 SSB-1200's in trade for 18 SDP40F'S, all of which were surplus on both roads.

Santa Fe's Public Relations Department can be very obliging, and on September 10, 1985, they mustered together four cowl units for the 1-199-08 train for a feature article in Railfan Magazine. The units involved were 5257-5954-5950-5986 (SDF40-2/ 3 SDF45's), with the train being handled by Road Foreman of Engines Homer Henry, with author/photographer David Lustig in the fireman's seat. *Mike Martin/SFSP Corp.*

The 885 train (LA-Texas) is just west of Devore, California, on May 3, 1986, powered by 5256-5330-red 5335-5173 (SDF40-2/2 SD45's/SD40-2). The SDF40-2's do not usually operate on the point, as the crew must change via the steep side door making a rolling crew change impossible. *Joe Shine*

97

SDP45

None of SP's SDP45's have been rebuilt, so it was surprising that three of the ten, two passenger and one freight, had been repainted in the merger scheme. Freight unit #3208 leads a West Colton-LA hauler out of Colton on May 3, 1986. *Joe Shine*

Most of the freight SDP45's, such as the 3209 (left), have been working the haulers out of West Colton, usually grouped together or with SD39's.
Frank Keller
After being replaced on the Bay Area commute runs by CalTrain F40PH's, the SDP45's returned for a brief period due to braking problems with the new passenger units during the late summer of 1985. Below #3203 assists CalTrain #909 and three cars at Santa Clara.
Paul Lukens

SDP45 CONTINUED

SOUTHERN PACIFIC SP 3200,02-06,08-09
(SPSF 6406-6413)

Southern Pacific's once extensive passenger fleet of Alco PA/PB's and EMD E-units were nearing the end of their careers in the mid-1960's when a decision was made to augment their remaining mainline passenger units. When the SDP45's were delivered in June 1967, SP's passenger roster contained only ten Alco PA's (all PB's were already gone), two E7A's, one E8A, nine E9A's, seventeen FP7's, plus quite a few F7 A&B units which could be used in passenger service. Ten GP9's, a pair of SD9's, along with sixteen Fairbanks-Morse Trainmasters held down the San Francisco-San Jose commute pool at that time.

EMD had already built two types of C-C passenger hood units, SDP35's and SDP40's, neither of which had been purchased by Southern Pacific. SP opted for the larger 3600hp SDP45's which originally replaced the few remaining Alco PA's on the Overland Route.

The SDP45's have had very interesting careers over the past nineteen years. They began on mainline passenger runs, powering such trains as the "City of San Francisco", the "Cascade", the "Lark", and the "Coast Daylight". Five were leased by Amtrak during their early years and plied the rails between Los Angeles and Portland on the "Coast Starlight". They replaced the aging Trainmasters on the demanding commute runs, and when not in use in that pool during weekends and holidays, they were used in freight service. Mechanically, they are identical to the freight SD45, and for that reason since being displaced from the commute pool by CalTrains' F40PH-2 units, they are now working strictly freight.

None of the ten SDP45's have been rebuilt, and as of this writing, SP 3205 has been the only one set aside.

SOUTHERN PACIFIC SP 3201 & 3207
(SPSF 7900-7901)

A pair of SDP45's, SP 3201 and 3207, are being held as passenger equipped units for business car specials or whenever steam boiler equipped units would be needed. It was believed that the SPSF would retain these two units as standby passenger units also, thereby placing them in a separate numbering series.

Presented here are two photos with SDP45 #3201 on the point. To the left, in November 1985, both passenger units (3201 and 3207) are westbound near Beaumont, California, enroute to Sacramento to be painted in the new merger red and yellow. Below, less than one month later newly painted 3201 assists Amtrak's "Coast Starlight" into San Luis Obispo.

Mike Start

Paul Lukens

SD45

During the holiday season extra passenger equipment fill out most consists, and more motive power is needed. To help fill this need home road units are usually leased by Amtrak to help keep the trains on the advertised. During the Christmas season in 1985, SP obliged Amtrak with newly painted SD45R's and SDP45's 3201 and 3207, but on December 24th unrebuilt SD45 #8981 leads the "Coast Starlight" into San Luis Obispo——on time, we might add!
Paul Lukens

Although Farr air intake shields and exhaust fins have been used extensively on Santa Fe motive power, it is very rare on the Espee. Until recently SD45 #8818 was the only locomotive so equipped, however a few Roseville assigned GP38-2's now carry this equipment.
Joe Shine

During the summer months unit sugar beet trains are familiar in California's central valley, and on the Coast Line. At Burbank Junction SD45 #8910 is in charge of four "big units" as the train crosses over to head up the coast.
Mike Martin

SD45 CONTINUED

SOUTHERN PACIFIC
COTTON BELT
SP/SSW 8818-9155*
(SPSF 6300-6408)

Southern Pacific entered the high horsepower market in 1966 by placing an initial order for forty-five EMD 3600hp SD45's. More orders followed shortly, and by the spring of 1968 the SD45's were numbered SP 8800 through 8963. The next order was purchased for the St. Louis Southwestern (Cotton Belt), and carried numbers SSW 8964-8981. There were more orders divided between Espee and the Cotton Belt, with the delivery of the last SD45 #9155 being received in January 1970, for a total of 356 units.

A wreck-damaged SSW 8971 was rebuilt by EMD in 1971, and reentered service as SSW 9156. Likewise, SP 8908 and 8857 were shopped and renumbered SP 9136(2nd) and 8992(2nd) respectively.

Many unrebuilt SD45's have been retired, and there are just over 100 left, of which many are stored awaiting disposition.

SOUTHERN PACIFIC
SP 7400-7566
(SPSF 6600-6766)

The rebuilding program for Espee's "big" EMD power (SD40's and SD45's) began with the shopping of the 8809 in 1979. The prototype, #7400, was outshopped during mid-December and was the last SD45 rebuilt until the 7300 series SD40's were completed. The SD45 GRIP program was begun again in mid-1981, with the 7401 entering service in September. The SD45's were rebuilt through the first quarter of 1986 with the last unit to go through Sacramento being the #7566. Between 1981 and 1986 a total of 167 SD45's were upgraded with their original 20-cylinder engines. The prime movers of SP 7400 through 7536 were derated by 400hp to reduce stress thereby improving reliability of their 20/645 engine. The units 7537 and above retain their 3600hp due to improved assemblies offered by EMD. Beginning in the second quarter of 1986 Espee turned to the more economical rebuilding of their SD45T-2's, which began the GRIP II program.

SOUTHERN PACIFIC
SP 7399
(SPSF 5500)

One lone SD45, SP 7399, was rebuilt with a new 16-cylinder 3000hp prime mover, making it essentially a SD40 in a SD45 carbody.

Just east of Bakersfield at Edison a helper set waits to assist an eastbound freight through the Tehachapis. If you pay attention every once-in-a-while you may catch an oddity, such as Cotton Belt SD45 #9155 with "SP" initials on its nose, definitely not the norm.
Joe Shine

By the first of year (1986) Sacramento Locomotive Works was turning out quite a few units in the new merger paint scheme. Prior to being released to service three freshly repainted units rest in the afternoon sun. SD45 #9128 was one of the last units to be painted in the old gray and red, while merger painted SD40T-2 #8286 and SD45 #9098 show off their new bright scheme.
John L. Shine

SD45 CONTINUED

SP #7399, at West Colton in January 1986, is the only SD45R equipped with a 16 cylinder prime mover. It was originally painted in the "Daylight" red, orange and black, until late in 1985, when it entered Sacramento for shop work and emerged in the merger red and yellow. *John L. Shine*

Los Angeles assigned SD45R #7430 is in Beaumont helper service in May 1986, and is waiting in the helper pocket at Loma Linda, east of Colton, to assist an eastbound as far as West Palm Springs.
James R. Doughty

SD45R #7562 at Mojave on May 1, 1986, displays an interm version of the merger scheme. It still carries SP style large cab numbers, but the oscillating lights have been removed.
John L. Shine

Does SD45R #7564 display things to come? If the merger is eventually approved SP locomotives will not have the larger cab numbers, or Mars-lights, but will have the rotary beacon on the roof. The date is May 1, 1986, and the 7564 is leaving West Colton on a westbound freight. *John L. Shine*

102

SD45 CONTINUED

Santa Fe's SD45 rebuild program began in January 1980, with the 5300 and 5426 classes. The 5300 class kept their original 20-cylinder engines, while the first four units of the 5426 class were reengined with 16-cylinder prime movers. The 5300 poses at San Bernardino on March 18, 1986, much the same as it appeared more than six years ago when rebuilt.
Thomas A. Chenoweth

SANTA FE

ATSF 5300-5404*
(SPSF 7000-7102)
ATSF 5426-5437
(SPSF 6950-6961)

Santa Fe's initial purchases of EMD's 3600hp SD45's, from two back-to-back orders, was rather impressive with 90 units (1800-1889) being delivered between June and December 1966. However, unlike the Espee, Santa Fe did not go back for large acquisitions, but rather purchased twenty-five (5590-5614) in April and May 1969, and the last group (5615-5624) which arrived in June 1970. Concurrent with the delivery of this last group of SD45's the original group was renumbered in the 5500 series.

During 1980 the remanufacturing program for the SD45's proceeded in three groups. The first, 5300-5303, were upgraded with their original 20-cylinder prime movers, and outshopped during March and April. A second group, 5426-5429, outshopped in May and June, were upgraded with new 16-cylinder engines rated at 3500hp. These first eight locomotives were rebuilt at the San Bernardino Shops, while the third group, 5496-5499, were rebuilt with Sulzer engines from Switzerland at Morrison-Knudsen's Boise, Idaho shops. These M-K rebuilds were returned to the Santa Fe for service during the first half of 1981. After comparative testing with the 5300, 5426 and 5490 classes the remanufacturing program proceeded with the much less expensive 5304 class which retained their original engines. Between March 1981 and July 1982, eight more SD45's, 5430-5437, were rebuilt with new EMD 16-cylinder 16-645F3 engines, but replacing the troublesome 20-cylinder prime movers was deemed too expensive and that program was terminated. The remanufacturing of SD45's into the 5304 class continued through 1985, with the last unit #5404 being outshopped during the third quarter.

As the painting of merger units progressed a few oddities have shown up. While many of Santa Fe's renumbered, but not repainted, GP35's and GP39-2's received red number boards, a few red and yellow units, such as SD45 #5362 above, received old style black number boards. This SD45 is also unusual as it is one of only a very few merger units equipped with Farr air intake shrouds and smoke deflectors.
John L. Shine

SD45 CONTINUED

Santa Fe's rebuilt SD45's in the 5426 class are very similar to SP's 7399, in that they both have been rebuilt with new EMD 16-cylinder prime movers. Here the class engine climbs toward Cajon Pass at Ono in February 1986.
Mark A. Denis

SD45 "B" UNITS   ATSF 5501-5502 (SPSF 6990-6991)

There were a couple of oddities within the SD45 rebuild program. A pair of unrebuilt 5500 series SD45's were rebuilt as cabless "booster" units. The short hoods were constructed at San Bernardino from scrapped Geeps purchased secondhand from a dealer. The thinking was that by eliminating the cab a number of control circuits could be eliminated thereby producing a more maintenance free locomotive. The two "B" units, 5501 and 5502, were outshopped concurrently with standard SD45 rebuilds 5375 and 5376 in December 1983, and "broke in" between Barstow and Los Angeles as an A-B-B-A set. After the break in period they were separated and assigned to Barstow in the general freight pool. One of these unique B-units, 5502, was lost from wreck damage on July 3, 1986, but was not yet officially retired as of July 24th, our roster date.

A decision has been made that any Santa Fe road unit receiving extensive front end damage is to be rebuilt without a cab. SD45 #5340 fit into this category, and during the summer of 1986 was in the San Bernardino Shops being rebuilt with the high nose from SP GP9 #2891, which was purchased from Chrome Locomotive. A wreck damaged 5334 will probably follow.

SULZER REBUILDS   ATSF 5405-5408 (SPSF 7103-7106)

The four M-K Sulzer rebuilds mentioned earlier could not meet the arduous demands imposed by railroading in the American West, so their engines were again replaced with standard EMD 20-cylinder prime movers. The 5499 emerged from the San Bernardino Shops in December 1984 as the 5408, while the 5496-5498 became the 5405-5407 respectively, during the summer of 1985. This concluded the rebuilding program for all of Santa Fe's 123 SD45's, except for wreck damaged units being rebuilt as B-units.

At press time (October 1986) the 5501 was the lone SD45 "B" unit, as the only other SD45B #5502 was destroyed in an accident on July 3, 1986. However, there is a second #5502 "B" unit which was rebuilt from SD45 #5340 and SP GP9 #2891 in the San Bernardino Shops, which will be outshopped during the fourth quarter of 1986. The 5501 is in an eastbound consist at Needles, California in March 1986.
Charlie Slater

The two original SD45B units, 5501 and 5502, were outshopped simultaneously with regular SD45's 5375 and 5376. As with all newly released units, at first, they are kept close to home, as we see the 5376-5501-5502-5375 enroute to Barstow near Oro Grande in October 1983.
Joe Shine

104

SD45 CONTINUED

On September 9, 1985, red #5401 leads blue 5400 and red 5394 along with six more blue units and three business cars toward Barstow from San Bernardino in a power move, common in this area on Sundays and Mondays due to the traffic flow.
Gail Shine

Santa Fe 5405 was built in 1966 as the 1841, renumbered in 1970 to 5541, and was chosen as one of four SD45's to be remanufactured with a Swiss built Sulzer prime mover in February 1981, installed by Morrison-Knudsen. It was returned from M-K's Boise, Idaho, shops as the 5496, but the Sulzer engines were too expensive to maintain, and EMD 20-cylinder engines were reinstalled at San Bernardino in 1985, with the 5496 becoming the 5405.
Joe Shine

Red and yellow SD45 #5331 ran for a time as a test bed for painted trucks. The front truck was painted in the standard silver, while the rear truck was gray. Sporting this oddity the 5331 was photographed on the point of the 971 train on the mainline between the pair of sidings at Woodford in the Tehachapis on April 19, 1986.
John L. Shine

105

SDF45

SANTA FE ATSF 5950-5989
(SPSF 6550-6589)

Santa Fe's forty freight cowl units, EMD F45's #1900-1939, were delivered in June and July of 1968, just six months after their passenger FP45's were put in service. Although these F45's contained a streamlined carbody they were painted in the standard freight scheme, blue with yellow trim.

During the 1969/1970 renumbering program these F45's were renumbered 5900-5939. To help supplement the passenger FP45's, twenty F45's, 5920-5939, received steam and signal lines, and were usually operated as trailing units in passenger consists, both prior to Amtrak and as leased to Amtrak.

The forty units were remanufactured concurrently with the SD45's, and FP45's at the San Bernardino Shops between January 1982 and November 1983, emerging as the 5950-5989, and redesignated as SDF45's.

Although the Great Northern, and later the Burlington Northern, had a sizable roster of F45's, only Santa Fe's are still intact.

Don Steen

It's mid-day at Caliente, California, (above) as an eastbound with SDF45 #5967 on the point holds the main as 5979 with a westbound takes the siding on April 27, 1985. Near Belen, New Mexico, (left) a five unit consist with SDF45's on each end rushes one of Santa Fe's hot "pig trains" toward its destination.
James R. Doughty

Merger painted SDF45 #5969 is picking up empty truck and auto carriers from the south main, a leaning curve at this point, at Buena Park, California, on April 23, 1986.
Joe Shine

106

SDFP45

SANTA FE

ATSF 5990-5998*
(SPSF 7990-7997)

Just months after Southern Pacific took delivery of their ten passenger SDP45's, Santa Fe ordered brand new streamlined passenger units from both EMD and GE. The nine EMD FP45's, #100-108, were delivered in December 1967, housed in a cowl-type carbody. These aesthetic units carried the famous silver with red warbonnet scheme, and at first were assigned mainly to the pride of Santa Fe's passenger fleet, the combined Super Chief and El Capitan. During 1970 they were renumbered 5940-5948 with no assignment change. When Amtrak assumed operation of passenger trains in May 1971, these FP45's, along with the F45's, were assigned almost exclusively to the Super C, Santa Fe's fast Chicago-Los Angeles TOFC train. Then in January of 1973 Amtrak leased all of the 5940 class FP45's, along with a few 5900 class F45's, to fill in for the ailing F3/F7 fleet until their own SDP40F's were delivered during the summer of 1973. After the delivery of Amtrak's big cowl units, Santa Fe's FP45's and F45's were relegated strictly to freight duties on the Chicago/Kansas City-West Coast mainline.

These FP45's were rebuilt along with the SD45 and F45 fleets at San Bernardino Shops between 1980 and 1982. Upon being remanufactured they were renumbered 5990-5993 and 5995-5998, and redesignated as SDFP45's by the Santa Fe.

Only one of the original forty-nine cowl units has been retired. The 5944 was retired in 1981 prior to being upgraded.

History was made on April 12, 1986, when Santa Fe and Amtrak cooperated in providing a special passenger train celebrating the centennial of the high desert communities of Hesperia, Victorville and Barstow. With white flags flying (made by ATSF Historical Society member Rose Steen) SDFP45 #5998 and Amtrak F40PH #284 head for Barstow with stops at Hesperia and Victorville. *Don Steen*

During the late afternoon of February 23, 1986, the 179 train is about to enter tunnel #2 between Bealville and Caliente with 5996-5955-5979-5959, all red cowl units, plus one blue and yellow SDF45 at the rear of the consist. *Joe Shine*

107

SD45-2

SANTA FE

ATSF 5625-5704*
(SPSF 7200-7275)
ATSF 5705-5714*
(SPSF 7300-7308)

The first EMD dash 2 locomotives came to the Santa Fe in the form of 3600hp SD45-2's in May 1972, with the delivery of 5625-5661. These first thirty-seven units were followed one year later by a second order of forty-three, 5662-5704. While most other roads making major purchases of EMD six-axle road power opted for the less troublesome 16-cylinder 3000hp SD40-2's, the Santa Fe and Southern Pacific continued to go with the higher horsepowered SD45-2's. The Santa Fe purchased ten more the following year, in May of 1974, as the 5705-5714, for a total of 90 units.

The SD45-2's can be distinguished from their older SD45 cousins by a longer wheelbase and by non-flared radiator grills. Santa Fe's would have been the only regular SD45-2's entering the merger, as all of Southern Pacific's are the tunnel version SD45T-2's.

With the conclusion of the SD39 rebuild program (1556 series) at the San Bernardino Shops in February 1986, the SD45-2's were the next units to be remanufactured. During the second week of February the first rebuilt SD45-2 was outshopped as #7200.

Thirty had been rebuilt by July 24, 1986 (ICC decision day), #7200-7229, all in the SPSF red/yellow scheme. As the 7200 class was a SPSF series of numbers, it was decided to renumber all of the 7200's into the 5800 class, which are strictly Santa Fe numbers. This renumbering of previously rebuilt units began during the first week of August 1986. The next rebuilt SD45-2 outshopped was #5830, which was painted in the familiar blue/yellow warbonnet scheme. The 7205 was shopped during most of July and August due to accident damage and was the first unit in merger paint to be repainted into the blue and yellow scheme.

Due to the fact that #5644 and 5658 were retired in 1977, the 5687 was retired in 1980, and a red and yellow 5694 in 1986, there are only 76 SD45-2's to be remanufactured.

The group acquired in May 1974, #5705-5714, are leased and are not scheduled to be rebuilt at this time. Of this later group the 5706 was retired in 1980.

The westbound 358 train passes the Vaughn, New Mexico depot in June 1985, headed by SD45-2 #5629. Just west of this location there is a new interchange between the Santa Fe and Southern Pacific.
James R. Doughty

The 971 train led by a pair of units equipped with air intake shields and smoke deflectors, SD45-2 #5713 and SD45 #5336 plus GP40X #3808, work upgrade through Woodford, toward Tehachapi, on the mainline in July 1985.
Mike Martin

SD45-2 CONTINUED

A few SD45-2's such as the 5682 at San Bernardino on December 3, 1985, were painted in the merger red and yellow just prior to being retired for rebuilding into the 7200 class.
John L. Shine

Rebuilt SD45-2 #7216 at Mojave on July 3, 1986, is crossing over to leave the Southern Pacific track and is about to head across the desert bound for Barstow on home rail.
Joe Shine

Since the merger denial by the ICC in July 1986, the SPSF 7200 class was being changed to the Santa Fe 5800 class. One of the first to be renumbered was the 5824 (old 7224) photographed in helper service at Walong in August 1986.
Don Steen

Beginning with SD45-2 rebuild #5830 all units painted at San Bernardino were released in the familiar blue and yellow scheme. In August 1986, blue 5831 is followed by rebuilt SD45 #5333 in red, at Cable, just west of the city of Tehachapi.
Don Steen

109

SD45T-2

Santa Fe's 971 train is in the long siding at Woodford while a westbound SP freight lead by SD45T-2 #9224 is in dynamics on the main which is the middle track on September 21, 1985.
Mike Martin

Mike Start

EMD's tunnel motor version of the SD45-2 is identical to the regular SD45-2 to a point just behind the dynamic brake blister as noted in the photo (above) of SP 9227. Freshly painted SD45T-2 #9254 idles in the helper spur at Bena, just east of Bakersfield in February 1982. All the SD45T-2's are identical with the exception of the lack of air conditioners on earlier orders.
Joe Shine

An interesting comparison may be made from this photo of the length difference of SD45 SP 8950 and SD45T-2 SSW 9265, between Walong and Woodford in January 1984.
James R. Doughty

SD45T-2 CONTINUED

SOUTHERN PACIFIC SP/SSW 9157-9404*
COTTON BELT (SPSF 7600-7834)

A type of diesel unique to the Southern Pacific and Cotton Belt is the EMD SD45T-2, which is the tunnel motor version of the 3600hp SD45-2. The dash 2 models contain much hardware which was first tested on the EMD and SP SD45X units of 1970. They contain a modular solid state electrical control system and are equipped with larger D87 traction motors in redesigned trucks.

Unlike the SP SD40T-2's, which came later, none of these SD45T-2's were ordered with large noses or snoots. All of the unrebuilt 45T-2's are nearly identical, with oscillating light packages only on the nose.

The 247 units were delivered between February 1972 and June 1975. The groups 9157-9165, 9261-9301 and 9371-9404 are all Cotton Belt, while all in between are Southern Pacific. The damaged SP 9220 was rebuilt and emerged from the shops as SP 9314 in 1974. The 9174, 9205, 9210, 9216, 9354 and 9379 have been retired, and because of high mileage, many of the more troublesome units have been stored serviceable, only to be called to duty during extreme shortages of motive power. More have been set aside recently for the Grip II program, so the ranks of the SD45T-2's are slowly dwindling.

Only one, the bi-centennial Cotton Belt #9389, was ever painted other than the gray and scarlet, until 1986 when a few were painted in the SPSF red with yellow bonnet scheme.

Due to the fact that these units already have the dash 2 components, it was deemed much more economical to start the program to rebuild these SD45T-2's instead of continuing to rebuild the older SD45's, which would stretch the maintenance dollar much further.

SOUTHERN PACIFIC SP (9500)-9501
 SPSF 6767,6769-6771

The first SD45T-2R in the new Grip II program was outshopped by the Sacramento Locomotive Works on April 28, 1986 followed by the second exactly one month later. These first two were originally numbered SP 9500 and 9501, strictly Southern Pacific numbers, which conflicted with Santa Fe's own rebuilding of U36C's into the post merger 9500 class. The SPSF planners had a different schedule which called for all new SP rebuilds to be renumbered in the new SPSF series. This meant that the new rebuilds would be renumbered behind the rebuilt SD45's beginning at 6767 (SP's SD45 rebuilds were to be renumbered SPSF 6600-6766). In early June the 6769 was outshopped, and later that month the 9500 was renumbered 6767. With the ICC's disapproval announcement on July 24th, Espee's numbering and/or renumbering was put on hold before the 9501 could be renumbered. The 6770 was released during July in merger paint, while the 6771 came out during August in gray and red.

Cotton Belt SD45T-2 #9263 leads an impressive consist of SP/SSW and Rio Grande power east of Tucson, Arizona, in August 1984. Yes, that second unit mixed with the big power is SSW 4149, a rebuilt GP20. *James R. Doughty*

SD45T-2 CONTINUED

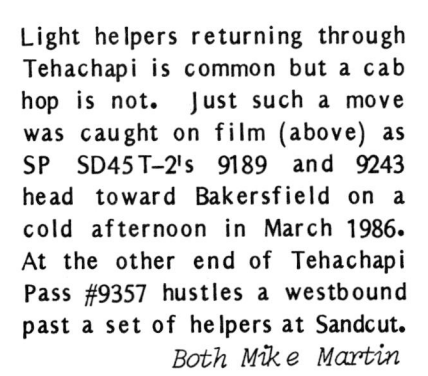

Light helpers returning through Tehachapi is common but a cab hop is not. Just such a move was caught on film (above) as SP SD45T-2's 9189 and 9243 head toward Bakersfield on a cold afternoon in March 1986. At the other end of Tehachapi Pass #9357 hustles a westbound past a set of helpers at Sandcut.
Both Mike Martin

Repair work is performed as needed on units when they are off line, and that may be the reason for the Union Pacific style numbers in the numberboard on SD45T-2 #9367. Note also that the air conditioner has been removed which make the horns appear much higher.
Mark A. Denis

While in for routine maintenance quite a few non-rebuilt SD45T-2's were painted in the merger scheme, such as the 9338 caught at Industry, California, in August 1986. *John L. Shine*

SD45T-2 CONTINUED

Unrebuilt SD45T-2 #9350 at Mojave differs from the 9338, page opposite, in that the classification lights on the nose have been plated over.

John L. Shine

Some of the units awaiting a berth at the Sacramento Locomotive Works were painted in the merger scheme, then stored until the shop could handle them. SD45T-2 #9192 is outside of the shops at Sacramento on July 19, 1986, just six days before the ICC handed down their decision.

John L. Shine

Tunnel motor #9163 became SP's prototype GRIP II SD45T-2 rebuild in early 1986. Outshopped as SP 9500 (strictly an SP number) while Santa Fe had been renumbering their rebuilds in the post-merger scheme. Photographed on June 14th, by months end it had been renumbered SP 6767, a post-merger number. The only other rebuilt SD45T-2 released in the 9500 series, #9501 (below), was photographed at Mojave on September 1, 1986.

John L. Shine

Don Steen

113

U25B

SOUTHERN PACIFIC
**SP 3100
(SPSF 1599)**

In September 1975 and September 1976, Espee rebuilt two 2500hp GE U25B's in the GRIP program which was, in time, deemed too expensive. The 1963-built units originally numbered 7508 and 7524 became 6708 and 6724 in 1965, and upon rebuilding became U25BE's 6800 and 6801. In June 1979, the 6800 was renumbered SP 3100 for West Colton-LA drag freight service, and because of engine problems the 6801 did not become 3101 until July 1981. The 3101 was subsequently retired, while the 3100 has been stored serviceable and was to be designated SPSF 1599.

Southern Pacific GE U25BE #3100 has been stored serviceable for a number of years, but was assigned a SPSF number, and so is included here. In as much as it is a one of a kind unit, chances are that it would not have lasted long with the merged roads. In better days it was photographed at Taylor Yard, on March 19, 1980.

U23B

SANTA FE
**ATSF 6300-6348
(SPSF 8100-8133)**

Between mid-1970 and early 1971 Santa Fe purchased forty-nine 2250hp GE U23B's. These medium horsepower units have served their entire careers working mostly on secondary trains and in local service on the Eastern and Western Lines. The ranks of these 6300 class units were greatly thinned in 1984 when fourteen were traded to General Electric for new C30-7's. The 6321 was retired in 1983, but there are still thirty-four U23B's on the Santa Fe, all of which are stored servicable.

The units on the roster during mid-1986 were the 6300, 6304-6305, 6309, 6311, 6313-6319, 6322-6323, 6325-6330, 6332-6338, 6340, 6342-6345, 6347 and 6348.

Santa Fe U23B #6316 would be a very interesting unit for a model railroader to model as it is definitely different. Unlike the other U23B's it does not have a snowpilot, and it is air conditioned. *All Mark A. Denis*

One GE U23B was retired, and fourteen more were traded in on new C30-7's in 1983. The remaining units, like the 6309 at Kansas City in September 1985, were set aside during 1986, and according to all indications are slated to be rebuilt during 1987. With the apparent success of Santa Fe's U36C rebuilding program which turned out an almost completely new locomotive, the 9500 class SF30C, Cleburne Shops were chosen to remanufacture these "little GE's".

B23-7

SANTA FE ATSF 6350-6404, 6405-6418
(SPSF 8134-8188, 8204-8217)

Of the eighty-four GE B23-7's which would have entered the merger, sixty-nine would have been from the ranks of the Santa Fe. They came from four orders beginning in April and May 1978 with the delivery of 6350-6363, the second group came between April and June 1979 as 6364-6389, followed by 6390-6404 in April 1980. Almost five years had elapsed before the last group of B23-7's were delivered as #6405-6418. Just as the U23B's, these 2250hp units are assigned to the flatlands of the Eastern and Western Lines.

The 6415 is from Santa Fe's final group of B23-7's, 6405-6418, which came in December 1984. Unlike all previous B23-7's, these new units lacked the plated over nose receptacles for warning lights, a safety feature ordered by Southern Pacific and Cotton Belt, but not Santa Fe.
John L. Shine

A trio of B23-7's bask in the sun at Topeka, Kansas, in July 1985. The 6381 (right) and 6415 (above) ride on trucks from traded-in U25B's and U23B's respectively. *Mark A. Denis*

Red and yellow B23-7 #6354, at Chicago on July 25, 1986, was purchased in 1978 and rides on GE Floating Bolster trucks, and is equipped with a nose mounted air-conditioner. *John L. Shine*

Santa Fe B23-7 #6402 leads four GP20's past Emporia's Merrick Tower in August 1985. Both of these types of units normally work Santa Fe's Eastern and Western Lines, and were rarely seen in the far west, however during 1986 the GP20's have become more common on the Coast Lines where they are assigned to local jobs.
Mark A. Denis

B23-7 CONTINUED

SOUTHERN PACIFIC SP 5100-5114
(SPSF 8189-8203)

Delivered in June 1980, following Santa Fe's third group, the Southern Pacific took delivery of their first and only GE B23-7's. There are no Cotton Belt B23's, however all fifteen, SP 5100-5114, are assigned to Pine Bluff, Arkansas (SSW territory). These fuel-efficient, twelve cylinder units lack silencer baffles over the radiator grills which was the norm for B30's and B36's delivered about the same time.

The 5110 has worked the way to West Colton in November 1985, and is being readied for a return trip to Pine Bluff, Arkansas.
James R. Doughty

During the night of July 14, 1986, B23-7 SP 5112, GP9's SP 3791 and 3368 along with GP20E SSW 4135, arrived at Pine Bluff from East St. Louis, a portion of which is on MP trackage. *John L. Shine*

Like Santa Fe's B23-7's, Southern Pacific's are usually to be found on the eastern end of the system. However during a shortage of motive power in late 1985, a few "little GE's" did manage to migrate west, such was the case with the 5114 at West Colton in December 1985.
Mike Start

B30-7

SOUTHERN PACIFIC SP 7801-7883*
(SPSF 8300-8380)

The first strictly freight B-B units purchased by the Southern Pacific in nearly twelve years arrived between January and April 1978, as SP 7800-7823. These 3000hp General Electric B30-7's were the first on the Espee to come equipped with the Floating Bolster (FB-2) truck and new wheel-slip controls. They were actually a new version of an old model, the U30B, which neither the Southern Pacific or Santa Fe purchased.

They were ordered about the same time as SP's first EMD GP40-2's, however unlike the GP40-2's, which had roof mounted air conditioners, the GE's came with air conditioners mounted in the nose section.

Sixty more identical B30-7's, SP 7824-7883, came between March and June 1979. Three have been retired, 7800, 7810 and 7857.

COTTON BELT SSW 7774-7799
(SPSF 8381-8406)

Cotton Belt's first GE's, four B36-7's SSW 7770-7773, and twenty-six B30-7's SSW 7774-7799, came between February and April 1980. They differed from SP's B30-7's as this group was equipped with roof mounted air conditioners, air intake baffles, and exhaust silencers which required a slightly larger stack.

A pair of SP B30-7's are switching the Fordyce & Princeton Railroad interchange, past the ex-Rock Island depot, at Fordyce, Arkansas on July 15, 1985. *John L. Shine*

SP B30-7 #7859, at LA on October 5, 1986, is one of the very few units painted in the merger paint scheme at Cotton Belt's Pine Bluff, Arkansas shops. This unit carries SP style number boards, but has Santa Fe style cab numbers. *Richard Fischer*

Cotton Belt B30-7 #7774 and a SP SD45 have just passed a westbound as they run long-hood-first on an eastbound freight east of Industry, California. Only Cotton Belt B30-7's and B36-7's and Santa Fe B36-7's came with air intake baffles, and Santa Fe has removed theirs. *Mark A. Denis*

117

B36-7

COTTON BELT SSW 7770-7773
(SPSF 8500-8503)

The first GE's owned by the Cotton Belt arrived in February 1980 as B36-7's, SSW 7770-7773. They were originally classed along with B30-7's SSW 7774-7799, which were in the same order. These B36's were initially rated at 3600hp during an extensive test period to evaluate them against data acquired from EMD's GP40X's in 1978. They were then derated to 3000hp to conform with the rest of the class. After the purchase of SP's B36-7's, these four units were again reclassified as B36-7's and rated along with Espee's units at the higher horsepower. The only external distinguishing feature on these B36-7's is an exceptionally large exhaust silencer stack. Internally they featured a new motor, generator and wheel-slip system rendering them far superior to previous General Electric models. In April 1981 the 7771 was involved in an accident which completely demolished its cab. It was rebuilt at Los Angeles as a cabless "B" unit with no number change. It was to become SPSF #8500.

SOUTHERN PACIFIC SP 7754-7769
(SPSF 8520-8535)

Late in 1984, a power hungry Southern Pacific took delivery of sixteen new GE B36-7's, SP 7754-7769, rated at 3750hp. These high horsepower units contain the latest wheel slip technology, and are usually found working east of Los Angeles with older GE B-B units and the many EMD GP40-2's. These units have slightly larger fuel tanks than Cotton Belt's original B36-7's, 3500 gallons compared to 3100.

Mark A. Denis

Cotton Belt B36-7 #7770 is on the point of a westbound freight on the Cotton Rock, Rock Island's old Golden State Route. Centralized Traffic Control is not in effect on this line, and as seen here, turnout switches must be hand thrown.

John L. Shine

On February 13, 1986, Cotton Belt B36-7B #7771 was on the SP, but during September and October 1984, this unique unit was working on the Santa Fe paying back horsepower hours owed. Below, on August 24, 1985, new B36-7's, SP 7769 and 7768 power the "Sun Sprint" through Beaumont Pass enroute to Phoenix from Industry.

Joe Shine

B36-7 CONTINUED

Arriving at Industry on a warm afternoon in May 1985, with the "Sun Sprint" from Phoenix is a pair of B36-7's SP 7761 and 7775. *Mike Start* Below, the AXAVT (APL double stack trailer train) with 5 B36-7's, SP 7756-7757-7762-7766-7763, is leaving Industry bound for New Orleans, on June 5, 1986. *John L. Shine*

When delivered, SP's B36-7's (7754-7769), were equipped with Nathen KH-5 horns fore and aft. They sounded great, but loud, and some crews refused to operate with them on the point so they were subsequently removed.

Joe Shine

119

B36-7 CONTINUED

SANTA FE
ATSF 7484-7499
(SPSF 8504-8519)

GE's second set of B36-7's, Santa Fe's first, (Cotton Belt received the original group), were delivered during October and November 1980 as 7484-7499. They, like the Cotton Belt units, have the large stack, and sound silencing baffles connected to the hand rails covering the air intake grills. Two of the units, 7484 and 7486, are set up as RCE (radio control) transmitters, with the 7485 and 7487 being receiver units, the first GE B36's to be so equipped. During the last couple of years they have usually been assigned to dedicated mainline power lashups with Santa Fe's other high horsepower B-B units, the GP40X's, GP50's and to a lesser extent, GE's B39-8's.

RCE master #7486 (note the small antenna plate near the rear of the unit) is stopped at Rivera, California, to make a setout of loaded autos with the 358 train, on June 8, 1986. The RCE equipment is located below the walkway behind the cab on the firemans side.
Joe Shine

Santa Fe positioned their brand new high horsepowered B-B units, GE B36-7 #7489 and GP50 #3817, together for their official portrait at Barstow in February 1981. Today these two types of units usually operate together on Santa Fe's fast TOFC and COFC trains. *SFSP Corp.*

On November 11, 1980, brand new B36-7's, 7492-7488-7493 make their first westbound trip, and have just made a crew change at San Bernardino. *Mark Denis*

SF30C

The first SF30C (rebuilt U36C), #9500, was caught on film in the unlikely company of 4679 and 4620, a pair of SD26's (Barstow switchers) on November 3, 1985. The 9500 was the only SF30C with nose classification lights, which have since been plated over. *Both John L. Shine*

SANTA FE ATSF 9500-9569 (SPSF 9500-9569)

Cleburne Shops has performed the first major rebuilding program initiated on a large class of General Electric units. The 3600hp U36C's, 8700-8705, 8707-8721, 8723-8735 and 8764-8799 are the first GE's to be remanufactured in a major program by any road. They have been redesignated as SF30C's with a 3100hp rating, and each unit has been completely disassembled and practically rebuilt from the ground up.

The external features consist of a completely new nose which is much narrower then that on the U36C, a larger extended exhaust stack, a bulge near the rear of the carbody to accommodate the main generator, duel fuel fillers (SP and ATSF types), and rear end vents. Internally they are equipped with the latest state-of-the-art technology, including GE's Sentry System wheel slip control, and complete new electrical systems, which include the relocation of the electrical cabinet to a much more accessible location, just behind the cab.

They are also unique for another reason, as they were the first group to be numbered for the then pending SPSF merger - the 9500's.

A number of SF30C's, including 9510-9532 (even) and 9511-9529 (odd), are equipped with the Locotrol II RCE master and receiver system for unmanned helper service.

Four 6-axle units led by red SF30C #9515 drift down hill toward San Bernardino with the 918 train on January 9, 1986. 9510-9530 and 9532 are set up as RCE masters and receivers equipped with Locotrol II. During May 1986, master 9518 and receiver 9513 were in use as instruction units for crews between La Junta, Colorado and Albuquerque, New Mexico, where they are scheduled to displace SD40-2 and C30-7 RCE units.

Sweetwater, Texas plays host to the 508 train powered by a U36C and SD40-2, on August 14, 1985.
Don Steen

April 5, 1986 finds an interesting group of units gathered on the ready tracks at Barstow. Red U36C #8752 is coupled to red SF30C #9522, while ex-Amtrak SDF40-2's 5250 and 5261 sit side-by-side in the background.
John L. Shine

Ten of the twenty-seven remaining U36C's were painted in the merger red and yellow as the 8744 photographed at Kansas City on April 20, 1986.
Thomas A. Chenoweth

U36C

SANTA FE   AT&SF 8736-8762
(SPSF 9400-9426)

Most of the system's largest General Electric locomotives, the U36C's, will not suffer the same fate as Santa Fe's earlier six-axle GE's, the 7500 series U23C's, and the 8500 series U33C's. Both types were returned to their lessor in 1984 after fifteen years of service.

Beginning in 1985 the first of these big 3600hp U36C's entered the Cleburne, Texas shops to be completely remanufactured, and reclassified as SF30C's in the 9500 series, a numbering group which fit into the general SPSF plan.

The first group to enter the shops for remanufacturing were from the original two orders of U36C's, 8700-8714, which were delivered in May and June 1972, and 8715-8735 which were delivered in March and April 1973. The third group, 8736-8762, delivered between May and July 1974, are leased and will not be rebuilt at this time. Many of this group were painted in the new SPSF red/yellow scheme.

These big GE's are not the favorite locomotives of many crews, but most of that has changed with the rebuilding. There were originally 100 locomotives in the 8700 class, but only 27 remain. Also there are only 70 rebuilt as SF30C's (9500-9569), as 8706, 8722 and 8763 were retired in 1981, 1977 and 1978 respectively.

Only twenty-seven GE U36C's remain (8736-8762) which were leased during the summer of 1974. On September 1, 1985, #8761 and three more units are in full dynamics as they ease a Bay Area bound train down hill and around the curves into Caliente.

Both John L. Shine

On May 14, 1986, SD40-2 #5067 with the First Sub Local holds the south main at Victorville, California, as the 881 train roars through on the north main with 8760-5043-5501-5253 (U36C/-SD40-2/SD45B/SDF40-2). Sitting in the pocket are Cajon helpers UP 3147-3190 (SD40-2's).

C30-7 CONTINUED

An all GE consist grinds uphill toward Cajon Summit from the east side with the 818 train (Barstow–LA) on May 3, 1986. Of the five units there are three different models represented. The consist; red 8032–6409–8751–8163–8043 (C30-7/B23-7/U36C/2 C30-7's).   *Joe Shine*

At milepost 2 on the Los Angeles Division/Third Subdivision, just west of San Bernardino, on March 8, 1986, the 918 train (empty "pig" flats for Hobart) also consists of a motive power move. This interesting lashup consists of; 8021–5328–5668–5958–5264–3849–7207–5960 (C30-7/SD45/SD45-2/SDF45/SDF40-2/GP50/rebuilt red SD45-2/red SDF45).   *John L. Shine*

On February 16, 1985 (above), the 188 train, a solid consist of ten-pack fuel foiler flats, is hurried through the eastern California desert at Amboy, between Needles and Barstow, by three GE C30-7's. The same day (below) three more C30-7's and a GP50 get the 991 train on a roll out of Needles toward the Arizona border.   *Both Joe Shine*

125

C30-7 CONTINUED

The last group of C30-7's delivered by GE (8153-8166) came without the plated over nose receptacle similar to the U36C's. The classification lights have been removed from 8156 leaving a very plain nose as compared to the earlier C30's. Gone also from this class when painted in the merger scheme is the odd (for Santa Fe) black numbers on white in the number boards. *John L. Shine*

On July 2, 1986, three C30-7's along with a SD45 and SD40-2, lift the 991 train around Tehachapi Loop at Walong. *Don Steen*

Merger painted C30-7 #8072 and GP30 #2735, taken at Argentine, Kansas, were photographed on a very historic day for the SFSP Corporation. July 24, 1986 was the date, and units painted after this date would revert back to blue and yellow for the Santa Fe, and gray and red for the Southern Pacific/Cotton Belt. *John L. Shine*

C30-7

SANTA FE   ATSF 8010-8166
(SPSF 9700-9854)

The largest group of General Electric locomotives which would have been on the merged system are the 3000hp C30-7's from the Santa Fe. There were 157 units which were purchased in seven orders beginning with the 8010 in December 1977, and ending in December 1982, with 8166.

They are in service systemwide on mainline freights and are also used extensively on heavy unit trains on home rails, as well as in power pools with the Burlington Northern on unit coal trains which terminate on Santa Fe rails.

Just days prior to the ICC decision in July, the first, and thus far only, C30-7 to be set aside, the 8067, was involved in an accident and was officially retired after our roster date.

At Scholle, New Mexico on August 21, 1985, C30-7 #8151 leads a pair of SD40's and an SD45, out of the picturesque Abo Canyon toward Mountainair.
Don Steen

The only 6-axle GE's equipped as RCE masters and receivers are Santa Fe C30-7's (masters 8138-8152/even, and receivers 8133-8151/odd. They are identifiable by the large blue "box" well behind the cab as on receiver unit 8135 at La Junta, Colorado, on June 2, 1985.
Mark A. Denis

Santa Fe's C30-7's are well represented by merger painted units, as exemplified by the 8086, at Walong in the Tehachapi's on a sunny August morning in 1986. The small plate to the right of the air conditioner is for the end-of-train-device antenna for trains operating without cabooses. *Don Steen*

123

U33C

SOUTHERN PACIFIC   SP 8585-8780*
(no SPSF numbers assigned)

General Electric products had been well represented on the Southern Pacific even prior to their first order, in late 1968, of big six axle U33C's. They owned a substantial roster of U25B's, plus U28B's, U28C's and U30C's.

General Electric's 3300 hp U33C's began making their apperance on the Southern Pacific in February 1969, with the delivery of the first thirty 8600-8629. Succeeding orders through 1974 placed the U33C numbering through SP 8796. Orders were placed for fifteen additional U33C's for 1975 delivery, and they were numbered in the 8585-8599 series (the 8800's were occupied by SD45's), bringing the total number of U33C's to 212 units. There were never any Cotton Belt 6-axle GE's.

All of the U33C's were originally assigned to Los Angeles for maintenance and operated in all directions out of L.A.

During the 1970's many types of SP motive power was assigned to operate in a locomotive pool with the Burlington Northern, between the Powder River Basin and the power plant at Elmendorf, Texas near San Antonio. However, after 1980 a group of U33C's were exclusively assigned to San Antonio for use in this SATX unit coal train. As age and maintenance problems began to plague this group the BN banned them from the power pool, and for many this was their last active assignment.

During the past few years only a small group of U33C's have been in active service and simultaneously a large number have been sold for scrap. There are 36 units left on the roster, of which most have been retired and await disposition. Eleven units have been active during the last couple of years due to periodic shortages of motive power. These units are the 8599, 8689, 8712, 8717, 8720, 8725, 8727, 8754, 8756, 8771 and 8777.

Southern Pacific U33C's are rather rare today with only a handfull left. One of the big GE's still active is the 8599 which is sitting alone at Beaumont, California, after being setout with a dragging brake shoe...nothing serious.
Joe Shine

In the middle of nowhere on the old Golden State Route (left) a power swap is being made with Cotton Belt B36-7 #7770 and SP U33C #8771 on the point during the summer of 1985.
Mark A. Denis

Below, an APL double stack train with 7769-8689-8263-8720-7821-7268 (B36-7/U33C/SD40T-2/U33C/B30-7/GP40-2) has just arrived at Industry and awaits permission to enter UP trackage to head toward Valla on April 22, 1986. *John L. Shine*

B39-8

SANTA FE   **ATSF 7400-7402 (SPSF 8800-8802)**

The third generation diesel made its debut on the Santa Fe in early 1984 with the delivery of General Electric's new B39-8 #7400, an RCE master. The second unit delivered, the 7402 came in September 1984, and in keeping with Santa Fe's policy of numbering RCE receivers as odd numbered units, the third B39-8, #7401 was built in December 1984.

They are without a doubt, the most sophisticated diesels on the roster, complete with GE's new computerized Micro-Sentry adhesion control system, along with several microprocessors on board for monitoring and control.

Other early purchasers of GE's new "dash 8" series include the Burlington Northern also with three, 16 cylinder, 3900hp B39-8's, Norfolk Southern (N&W) with fifty C39-8's, and Conrail with ten 3150hp C32-8's.

The 7400 tested on the Illinois Central Gulf Railroad for a brief period in 1984. It was returned to the Santa Fe, and during the first few months of 1985 the three ran together systemwide for evaluation. Then, during August of 1985, all three were traded to Conrail for three big blue C32-8's (CR 6617-6619) for testing and evaluation. The three were returned to the Santa Fe and are working in the general freight pool, usually with EMD GP40X's, GP50's and GE B36-7's.

On July 3, 1986, at Walong GE B39-8 #7402 leads four 6-axle units on the eastbound 991 train. Not long after this photo was taken all three B39-8's were turned over to the BN for testing.
Don Steen

GE's new dash-8 series, such as B39-8 #7402 at San Bernardino, present a uniquely different profile; a very rugged look. As an added note Norfolk Southern runs their C39-8's long hood first which, with this end, looks a bit odd. *Mark A. Denis*

In June 1985, the 7401 is arriving at San Bernardino in a consist with 6-axle power. When on the Santa Fe the three B39-8's usually work either together or with B36-7's, GP40X's or GP50's in the mainline freight pool.
Mike Start